GOT YOUR BACK

Helping Christian Men Forge The Brotherhood
Connections They Need

DR. GARY YAGEL

Endorsements

"Sometimes one comes across a book that is so profoundly true and arresting that it changes the way one looks at the world and, more important, how one looks at one's own life. I'm a loner. I could do the monastery thing if they would let me bring my wife. But a long time ago I found out that I simply can't do this by myself and was drug kicking and screaming into community. Now that move (a good one, I've found) has legs. Those "legs" are in Gary Yagel's book, *Got Your Back*. Read this book and rejoice in its truth. Then give it to every guy you know. We could change the world… but we can't do it alone."

Steve Brown, Founder of Key Life Ministries,
author, seminary professor

"One of the greatest reasons men get into trouble is that they don't have to answer to anyone for their lives. Ask around. You will learn that very few men have built accountability into their lives. It is the missing link of Christianity. Now Gary Yagel has written a new book to challenge men to recover this missing connection to other men. In *Got Your Back*, he makes a compelling biblical case that God never intended for Christian men (or women) to fight their spiritual battles alone. With the shoe-leather realism that comes from over thirty years discipling men, Gary supplies the biblical examples, real-life stories, and practical wisdom to inspire the men of your church to forge the brotherhood bonds they need for encouragement and accountability. This ten-week Men's Study is a valuable tool for every church's men's ministry tool box!"

Patrick Morley, PhD, Founder and Chairman of
Man in the Mirror, author, Bible teacher

"What a valuable book! With the patience and care of a soul-surgeon, Gary Yagel cuts through the layers of isolation that have immobilized so many Christian men, and expertly explains the cure. Want to wake up the men in your church? This little book — logical, biblical, spiritual, practical — is a great place to start."

Nate Larkin, Founder of the Samson Society, author of
*Samson and the Pirate Monks: Calling Men to
Authentic Brotherhood.*

"Gary Yagel knows men. He knows our hopes, dreams, temptations and struggles. In his newest book he shares keen insights about why we need each other and how we are to do life together in light of the power and freedom of the gospel. Contrary to the psychologized bromides of Dr. Phil, Oprah and other moral therapies, Gary delivers solid, biblical wisdom about living according to the redeemed masculine identity we have in Christ. Read this book and be encouraged!"

Dave Brown, Director and Pastor at Large of the
Washington Area Coalition of Men's Ministries, Washington, D.C.

"The picture of rugged individualism is a dangerous myth that is as American as apple pie and has been portrayed in the movies by everyone from John Wayne to Bruce Willis. Far too many Christian men have bought into this deathly myth and crashed and burned. The followers of Jesus are not called to independence nor are they doomed to a life of dependence/co-dependence. We are instead called to a third, higher way, one of interdependence. This is the great truth skillfully laid out in Gary Yagel's new book, *Got Your Back*. This straightforward, no-nonsense book identifies the problem that far too many Christian men in today's church face and what to do about it. A must read for all men to desire to be faithful Christ-followers."

Hugh Whelchel, Executive Director of the Institute for
Faith Work and Economics, author of *How Then Should We Live*

"In Christ' is our identity. 'Comrades in Christ' should be our stance as men facing spiritual and relational battles daily. Yet we often stumble not knowing how to scout out or form such mutual discipleship. Gary's book, *Got Your Back*, is a welcomed ambush: direct, incisive, practical drawn from solid biblical exposition. *Check 6* questions have proven essential for men who desire to be a combat buddy…in Christ."

Carroll Wynne, Minister of Pastoral Care,
Tenth Presbyterian Church, Philadelphia, PA

"The book, *Got your Back,* provides excellent illustrations and examples of men needing accountability in their lives. The spiritual battles that each one of us fights daily will leave us defeated without a close friend! This book compels the readers to focus on their lives and make adjustments and apply many of the principles given in an easy read outline."

J Nevin Gish, Men's Ministry Coordinator,
Westminster Presbyterian Church, Lancaster, PA

"Isolation is killing us men! In *Got Your Back* Dr. Gary Yagel powerfully proves why we men can't do life alone for very long, and survive. Why do 19 out of 20 guys have no close friends? Gary tells us and then urges us on to explore a whole new universe of living that the Gospel of Grace opens up for men who choose to have brothers to fight for and who will fight for them. Bad decisions always bite back hard, and one of the worst decisions Christian men make is to ignore community with other growing guys. Life is too short to learn everything by our own personal experience. The Church of Jesus Christ needs just the type of men described by my friend Gary Yagel, built by grace, forged as Christ followers with other men who have got their back!"

Dr. Pete Alwinson, Vice President of Leadership and Men,
Key Life Network, Orlando, FL

"We have been using this book and the material in it for the last two years, first with our men's leadership team and then with the broader men's ministry. What I love about *Got Your Back* is the emphasis on relationship, because I have found that there is no true discipleship without it. It's easier to teach a Bible study than to develop a relationship, but most of our men have plenty of head knowledge about the Bible; what they need are brothers close enough to them who will encourage them to live what they know. *Got Your Back* provides the how-to for building those relationships and we need that how-to. But for me, the greatest value of this book is that each time I go through it, I am inspired to work hard at cultivating these kinds of relationships for myself and for my guys. We men need more than information about discipleship; we need inspiration to develop the relationships where discipleship actually happens, and Gary supplies that inspiration in this book."

Trent Casto, Associate Pastor,
Covenant Church of Naples, Naples, FL

Just as training and team development are essential keys to our ministry, *Got Your Back* is the key to developing leaders. In the first edition, Gary's book has proven to countless men, the need to forge bonds of brotherhood. As church leaders call upon our ministry for training, I recommend this book as a first step toward building a strong leadership team. When Deacons, Elders, Pastors and men in general, have close friends/brothers; it is a win/win for the body of Christ. Up to date, relevant and practical, *Got Your Back* should be in your men's discipleship tool box."

Dave Enslow, Director of Next Steps for Men,
Regional Host of Iron Sharpens Iron, Sarasota, FL

Insightfully diagnostic and practically helpful; *Got Your Back* helped me understand some of my own struggles and gave me great tools to address them with grace. An important read for any man who longs to walk with Christ-like joy and integrity."

James Forsythe, Senior Pastor,
McLean Presbyterian Church, McLean, VA

"In *Got Your Back*, Gary Yagel addresses a common struggle found among men, especially in American culture. It is the struggle to overcome a hyper-independent spirit that can lead to lonely despair or moral failure. In this short booklet, he calls men to a biblical understanding of what it means to be male. Using vivid illustrations from real events or a military context, Gary demonstrates how men can develop healthy relationships of encouragement and mutual accountability, without compromising their masculinity. The Group Discussion questions provide a helpful catalyst to stir conversation and apply the principles covered in that chapter. *Got Your Back* promises to be a helpful resource for one-on-one or small group men's discipleship."

Dr. Stephen Estock, Coordinator of
Discipleship Ministries, Presbyterian Church In America

"The landscape of men's ministry is rapidly changing today away from the programmatic and organizational to the relational and organic. Pancake breakfasts and event-driven approaches no longer cut it when it comes to seeing the gospel intersect with and redemptively transform the lives of men. Today's man is looking for an authentic and applicable faith that can be lived out in side-by-side community with other men. *Got Your Back* is a study that puts feet to such a vision for men's ministry. Gary Yagel powerfully captures this necessary balance between the organizational and organic aspects of discipling men, lessons he has learned firsthand on the front lines. The study is challenging, insightful, practical, pertinent, and critically needed today for anyone seeking to seriously see Christ formed in the lives of men."

Tony Myers, Pastor of Spiritual Formation,
Northeast Presbyterian Church, Columbia, SC

GOT YOUR BACK

*Helping Christian Men Forge The Brotherhood
Connections They Need*

DR. GARY YAGEL

This book is dedicated to all those men who've had my back over the years: Steve Proia in high school, Al McCracken at Penn State, Jerry Benjamin while working for the government in DC, Rick Belliveau as we started Shady Grove PCA, Tom Webb and Tom Parker after whom my son is named, Mark Wennstedt who helped shape some of the ideas in this book, Bob Johnson who weekly encourages me, and Phil Fleming, my best friend. Thank you for loving me. Gary.

Contents

Introduction

———— ✳ ————

oday's church is experiencing an epidemic of male isolation. Research reveals that nineteen out of twenty Christian men have no best friend, no one helping them fight their spiritual battles, much less a brother who has their back.

Yet there are many signs that God's Spirit is at work, bringing the age of John Wayne Christianity to a close. Here are just three:

1. The rising generation of Christian men sees more clearly the importance of living out their faith in community. For some, the brokenness of their family of origin motivates them to seek connection in the family of God. Others realize that since sin has fractured the relationships of this world, the church is called to be the place where Christ's power to restore relationships is demonstrated. They are committed to building community, so that the church is seen to be a place where Jesus is reweaving the well-being (shalom) of his kingdom.

2. Twenty-first century Christian men are not particularly enamored with material success. Not only do they want to be engaged in a mission that matters, they also realize that their deepest struggles—with God, with themselves, with sexuality, with relationships—are spiritual in nature.

3. Today's rising generation of Christian men realizes that discipleship isn't a program; it's a relationship. They're not so much interested in a mentor or program that provides "The Ten Steps to Discipleship" as they are a brother (maybe an older one) who

1

walks with them through life's challenges as a Christ-follower. They want a brother saying to them, "Got your back."

In short, the conviction is growing among contemporary Christian men that God never intended for them to fight their spiritual battles alone. Way too conscious of the battles they are losing, today's men are wondering where to find a few close friends who will have their back. But **finding** them may be the wrong verb. They may need to **forge** them. This book is written to help men forge the kind of brotherhood connections they sense that they are missing, and know that they need.

The biblical principles you will discover in the subsequent pages are road-tested. Thousands of man-hours have been logged by men implementing these principles and churches executing these strategies, many of which first appeared in print eight years ago under the title, *Forging Bonds of Brotherhood*. This updated version, *Got Your Back,* has several new chapters that provide practical insights and strategies for using the material most effectively in your men's ministry. You will enjoy the varied stories of men who have moved out of isolation and into the kind of brotherhood connection experienced by Jonathan and David and by our Lord, with his close friends, Peter, James, and John.

Chapter 1

The Battle

A part of me loved war. Now please understand I am a
peaceful man, fond of children and animals. And I believe
that war should have no place in the affairs of men. But
THE CAMARADERIE our platoon experienced in that
war provides an enduring and moving memory in me.[1]

*S*cott was expecting the Iraqis to fire a few surface-to-air missiles
at his F-16 when he got close to his target, the nuclear power
plant south of Baghdad. What he wasn't expecting was an all out bar-
rage beginning twenty-five miles away. Screaming and cussing at the
SAMs that were exploding everywhere, Scott stayed on course, reached
his target, and dropped his bombs. But, as he pulled up, he could see
an SA3 explode right underneath his wingman's plane, blowing off his
fuel tanks and putting what later proved to be over a hundred holes in
the fuselage of his wingman's aircraft.

Miraculously, the pilot himself wasn't hit. Scott immediately flew to
his wingman's side, conducted a visual inspection of the damaged plane,
took over responsibility for his navigation and defense, and radioed for
help. He guided the damaged plane to the closest base for an emergency
landing, but bad weather made it impossible to land. For the next two
and a half hours, Scott worked feverishly, conducting emergency diverts
to refuel his wingman's plane to keep him in the air long enough to land
safely. The bad weather forced them to visit five different emergency

landing sites before they were able to get him on the ground. Scott literally saved his wingman's life.

A half hour after Scott had landed, a brigadier-general, who was one of the pilots on the mission, stopped by to visit Scott. In the general's words, "Scott was standing leaning against a bunch of sandbags, just holding on to them, and shaking like a leaf. He couldn't walk; he couldn't talk; he couldn't move anything. All he could do was stand there and shake. The guy had nothing left. All his adrenaline was gone. He gave everything he had that day for his wingman."[2]

Scott's heroic care of his wingman illustrates what all F-16 pilots know. You never fly alone. You need a wingman. You need another pilot in case you get into an emergency. You need someone watching your back—what pilots call their *six*—since a high percentage of aircraft are shot down by a threat they never see.

Everything about combat flying reinforces this principle. During the pre-flight brief, the pilot and wingman discuss tactics, techniques and procedures as well as the specifics of aircrew coordination. "When you're attacking the target, exposed to the threat, I will be above you, providing high cover, prepared to engage any threat that pops up. When you come off target, I'll roll in, expecting you to provide high cover for me. This is how we will communicate …" One of the most important parts of the brief is the discussion of emergencies—what will we do when the unexpected happens and things go bad?

After the brief, the aircrew walks to their jets for a pre-flight, reviewing the maintenance history of each other's aircraft, letting each other know what problems they could potentially have with the aircraft. Just prior to takeoff, the lead pilot and his wingman look over each others' jets very carefully to ensure that there are no problems: no doors open, no fluids leaking, flight control surfaces in the correct position for takeoff, etc. After their mission is completed, it is with each other that they carefully debrief.

The United States military is committed to the principle that in war, you cannot fight alone and survive very long. That is why our military trains as it does. Vietnam veteran Stu Weber recounts the words of his grizzled C.O. at the Army Ranger School at Ft. Benning.

> "Many of you will not complete the nine weeks. It is simply too tough. But, for those who do, when we are finished

with you, you WILL BE the U.S. Army's best. America's best. You WILL be confident. You WILL survive, even in combat. And you WILL accomplish your mission....

"Step one in your training is the assignment of your 'Ranger Buddy.' Difficult assignments require a friend. The two of you will stick together. You will never leave each other. You will walk together, run together, eat together, and sleep together. You will help each other. You will encourage each other. And as necessary, you will carry each other."[3]

Because our military understands that no man can fight alone and survive very long, the team is everything. In Mogadishu, Somalia, when the lead Blackhawk helicopter went down, a hundred Rangers formed a perimeter around the downed chopper and its pilot. In the ensuing firefight eighteen Americans were killed and seventy-five wounded. The Ranger code says you don't leave a fallen comrade to fall into the hands of the enemy.

In war no man can fight alone and survive very long. Yet that is the way Frank was fighting a fierce battle that raged inside his soul. He knew that the feelings he was experiencing with Pam, his secretary, were wrong, illicit. And yet he had never felt so wonderful in all his life. Pam loved him. Unlike his wife, Pam admired him. She understood him. She wanted him. Never had he felt so alive, so good—as he did when he was with her.

Yet, daily, he did battle with his conscience. Adultery was wrong. He knew that. As a pastor he had taught it. But to leave the warm embraces of a woman who deeply wanted him to return to the cold, almost hostile emptiness of his marriage was more than he could face.

His love for his wife had died a long time ago. He had realized that their feelings were dying, and almost mentioned his concerns to one of his church friends. But from the time he was a boy, Frank had been taught that men shoulder their own problems. He asked no one for help, and slowly his marriage decayed before his own eyes. He and Cindy simply focused more and more on their three kids and the house. Fights were more frequent. Affection cooled. Sex was rare until it finally became extinct. No wonder he couldn't control himself when Pam was so inviting.

The battle with his conscience grew even more intense when his and Pam's affair was discovered. He faced a mandate from his wife and the church. Break off with Pam and come back to Cindy or move out of the house, and face church discipline. Either, daily face the harsh anger of his wife, ridiculing him for his hypocrisy in a marriage where the feelings were completely dead or start over again with a new wife who loved him, admired him, and wanted him. He hated to damage his relationship with his kids who were fully grown by then. He loved them. But, the reality was, that relationship had already been severely damaged when they found out about the affair. As far as church discipline was concerned, he and Pam would solve that problem easily enough by simply leaving the church. He would have to leave the ministry to sell insurance, but life with Cindy, or life with Pam? Misery versus happiness? It was a no-brainer, regardless of the loud clamor of his conscience.

Frank divorced his wife, and moved in with his secretary, whom he married the day after the divorce was finalized. The repercussions of his decision were far reaching. His wife, despite the care of her adult children, would die a lonely and rejected woman. Since he had been the dominant influence as his kid's spiritual leader, his betrayal of his faith and their mother sent their faith into a tailspin. It would be over ten years before his youngest son, Jim, (then in his thirties) would come back to Christ. Frank's teen aged grandchildren were hurt even more severely. A blow was struck at the root of their confidence that Christianity was real. If Christianity was about hypocrisy and betrayal, why not dive headfirst into the pleasures of drugs, alcohol, partying, and illicit sex? So they did.[4]

Frank was taken down by temptation. His whole household crashed and burned, with the damage extending three generations. The parallel is obvious. The stakes are too high, the battle too fierce, the enemy too wily, the attacks too frequent, the cost of defeat too severe for any Christian man to fight his spiritual battles alone.

Many men miss this parallel because they don't view their everyday lives as a spiritual combat zone. Paul, however, says it is.

> *For we do not wrestle against flesh and blood, but against the rulers, against the authorities, against the cosmic powers over this present darkness, against the spiritual forces of evil in the heavenly places. Therefore take up the whole armor of God, that you may be able to withstand in the evil day, and having done all, to stand firm.* (Eph. 6:12-13)

Men are born to be warriors and Christian men are called to wage a fierce, three-front battle. We must daily battle the enemy within, our sinful nature, which relentlessly seeks to overpower us. Ever since the fateful day when Adam disobeyed God's command and ate the forbidden fruit, men have been conscious of this traitor that dwells in their hearts. John Owen describes this collaborator,

> However strong a castle may be, if a treacherous party resides inside (ready to betray at the first opportunity possible), the castle cannot be kept safe from the enemy. Traitors occupy our own hearts, ready to side with every temptation and to surrender to them all.[5]

It is true that in Christ, every believer has been made into a new creation, and indwelt by the Holy Spirit to transform our heart. But, we still must daily do battle with the sinful nature that remains. Paul describes this conflict,

> *But I say, walk by the Spirit, and you will not gratify the desires of the flesh. For the desires of the flesh are against the Spirit, and the desires of the Spirit are against the flesh, for these are opposed to each other...* (Gal. 5:16-17a)

Our own sinful nature is just one of the enemies we face daily. We must also resist a world that continually bombards us with enticements that seek to take the affections of our heart captive. Reformed Theological Seminary professor Steve Childers explains the sin that lies beneath most sins.

To Paul, mankind's root problem is not merely an external, behavioral problem—it is an internal problem of the heart. Paul believed that one of the primary reasons human hearts are not more transformed is because the affections of people's hearts have been captured by idols that grip them and steal their hearts' affection away from God.[6]

Such idols subtly propel us to do whatever it takes to get the success, respect, stimulation, financial stability, prestige, financial security, sexual pleasure, or "happiness" that our heart thinks it needs to be satisfied. So vulnerable is our heart to deception that Paul says the very thoughts that enter our mind need to be challenged. "For the weapons of our warfare are not of the flesh but have divine power to destroy strongholds. We destroy arguments and every lofty opinion raised against the knowledge of God, and take every thought captive to obey Christ…" (2 Cor. 10:4-5).

The third adversary to be engaged in this three-front war is a spiritual enemy who wants to "rob, and kill, and destroy" us and our loved ones (John 10:10). His name is Satan. He is on God's leash; but that does not mean that he and his cohorts do not have enormous power to destroy. Jesus was so aware of Satan's influence in this world that he taught his followers to pray daily, "Lead us not into temptation, but deliver us from the evil one" (Matt 6:13). On one occasion he said to Peter, "Simon, Simon, behold, Satan demanded to have you, that he might sift you like wheat, but I have prayed for you that your faith may not fail" (Luke 22:31).

If you are a Christ-follower, you have an adversary coming after you. John makes that clear in the book of Revelation. "Then the dragon (Satan) became furious with the woman (the church) and went off to make war on the rest of her offspring, on those who keep the commandments of God and hold to the testimony of Jesus" (Rev 12:17). John Eldredge is right when he argues,

Behind the world and the flesh is an even more deadly enemy…one we rarely speak of and are much less ready to resist. Yet this is where we live now—on the front lines of a fierce spiritual war that is to blame for most of the casualties you see around you and most of the assault against you.[7]

The spiritual warfare described in Scripture is not just a nice metaphor for the fact that life is sometimes difficult! It is reality. Yet the vast majority of Christian men are like Frank, fighting their spiritual battles by themselves. They have no one checking their six. Is it any wonder that so many are losing the battle with lust and pornography, the battle to be self-disciplined, the battle for the souls of their teens, the battle over whose values will shape our culture?

A few years ago I was standing in line to get some food at a men's "beast feast" where I was going to speak. The guy beside me said, "Gary it's not just in the military where fighting alone makes you vulnerable. That principle is true in the animal kingdom. If a pride of lions gets hungry for zebra steak, what do they do? They chase the herd until they can break one zebra away from the rest of the herd. Then they go in for the kill."

I responded, "And Scripture says, 'Your adversary, the devil prowls around like a roaring lion seeking someone to devour'" (I Peter 5:8).

Not long ago a survey was taken of over 120,000 Christian men, who were asked, "Do you have a best friend?" An astonishing ninety-five percent answered, "no."[8] *Nineteen out of twenty Christian men in our country are so disconnected that they have no best friend.* They have no comrade-in-arms.

It's not that Christian men today have no friends; it's that they have no friend close enough to have their back. Proverbs 18:24 is enlightening: "A man of many companions may come to ruin, but there is *a friend who sticks closer than a brother.*" Most Christian men today have many companions, but no friend who sticks closer than a brother. They have numerous *acquaintances*, but no *brothers-in-arms*.

With a friend who is merely an acquaintance conversation centers on the ball game, work, the kids, vacations, and the news—superficial subjects kept safely away from issues of the heart. "Acquaintance" and "superficial connection" are the concepts behind the Hebrew word used in the first half of Proverbs 18:24 which is translated, *companion*. In sharp contrast is having a true *friend*, (ESV), also translated, *beloved friend* who sticks *closer than a brother*.

This is the kind of brother Paul had in Epaphroditus. Paul introduced him to the Philippians as "my brother, fellow worker, and fellow soldier" (Phil. 2:25). Here are two souls knit together by common family bonds, by a common task to be accomplished, and by a common enemy to be faced. Epaphroditus was a true brother-in-arms to Paul, the kind every warrior needs. If Frank had had an Epaphroditus in his life, chances are that he never would have crashed and burned through his affair with Pam. His family would have been spared enormous pain.

What about you? Do you have a brother who knows where your spiritual battles rage, who is shoulder-to-shoulder with you fighting for you in prayer? Have you invited a brother into your life to be close enough to you so that he's got your back?

Group Discussion Guide

1. If one is *the pits* and five is *great*, pick a number for the kind of week you are having and tell why you picked that number.
2. If you had a best friend either as a boy or as an adult, describe that relationship.
    What caused you to be best friends?
3. What has been your past experience meeting with Christian men for Bible study?
4. How valid is the analogy made in this chapter between fighting a physical enemy alone and fighting spiritual enemies alone?
5. Which of the three spiritual battlefields—your sinful nature, the world, or the evil one—do we tend to ignore the most, in your opinion? Why?
6. Why do you think so many Christian men today have many acquaintances but no friend who sticks closer than a brother?

During the week: Think and pray about your answer to the question, "Do you have anyone in your life who knows where your spiritual battles are?"

Chapter 2

Why Do Nineteen Out of Twenty Christian Men Have No Best Friend?

How can a man learn to be a man, a husband, a father, a provider and protector—a full-orbed king, warrior, mentor, and friend? By walking with other men who are doing it. You learn to play ball by playing ball. And masculinity is a team sport. You and I, as men living in a tragically disoriented culture, need to experience the life-building of what Paul called a "brother, fellow-worker, and fellow-soldier." It is time we heed the call of the High King to His High Communion. It is time God's men come to his table in the round and, in the company of men, drink deeply of a fresh understanding of his kingdom and just what it takes to enjoy a man's role in it.[9]

No Christian man I know sets out to fight his battles alone. So, how did we get here? Why are nineteen out of twenty of us in this condition? Why has the church been so slow to grasp the reality that masculinity is a team sport? The survey that discovered that ninety-five percent of Christian men have no best friend also found that ninety-four percent had had a best friend at some time previously in their life. It is not that they *can't* experience a close-knit, best-friend relationship; it's that they *don't*. What are the obstacles to male connection that are imprisoning us in our isolation?

Difficulty with Intimacy

The first obstacle is that men typically find intimacy threatening. As someone has noted, most women can easily bare their souls but are quite modest when it comes to their naked bodies, while most men can easily bare their bodies but are quite reluctant to lay bare their *souls*. Men, by nature, are aggressive and competitive. They know intuitively that the number one rule of the jungle is, "Never show weakness, inadequacy, or fear." To reveal such vulnerability is to give the opponent an advantage. It is un-masculine.

David Smith in his classic work, *The Friendless American Male*, describes this innate, male resistance to transparency:

> Within each man there is a dark castle with a fierce dragon to guard the gate. The castle contains a lonely self, a self most men have suppressed, a self they are afraid to show....No one is invited inside the castle. The dragon symbolizes the fears and fantasies of masculinity, the left-over stuff of childhood.
>
> When men take the risk and let down the barriers (or drawbridge...) people respond to one another as whole persons and try to communicate with openness and intimacy. Openness brings with it opportunity for a growing relationship, for a wider range of deeply felt experiences. This is the stuff from which friendships are formulated and sustained.[10]

Ten-year-old David never read Smith's book; but he knew all about the dragon inside. One Sunday morning, he sat listening to his pastor's sermon, getting more and more convicted that he had not been reading his Bible as he should. The sermon came to a close with a prayer and a request from the pastor for all those who felt convicted to be in the Word more to raise their hands while the parishioner's eyes remained closed. David couldn't resist the temptation to open his eyes.

After the service, David said to his mom, "So you haven't been reading your Bible, huh."

She answered, "Did you open your eyes?" He admitted that he had.

Then she asked, "Did your dad raise his hand?"

"No."

"Did you raise your hand?"

"No."

"Don't you need to be reading your Bible more," she questioned.

"Yeah."

"Then why didn't you raise your hand?"

David responded, "Mom, I'm a guy. You don't expect Dad and me to bare our soul like you, do you?" Even ten-year-old David had a fierce dragon guarding his masculine heart to warn him about baring his soul.

This masculine, built-in resistance to vulnerability is magnified in men who took the risk to reveal something personal—some point of vulnerability, only to have it then used to embarrass or undermine them. They are exceptionally guarded about self-revelation and require a high dose of trust to disclose their soul.

An increasing number of men today have difficulty connecting with other men because they had no real relationship with their father. Fifty percent of the children growing up in America are wounded by the absence of a meaningful relationship with their dad. Thirty four percent grow up without their father physically present in their home. Another sixteen percent have no positive emotional bond with their dad. Either the emotional connection is harmful through abuse, or it is non-existent.[11]

In twenty-first century America, with the rising visibility of the gay lifestyle, there is an additional hesitation about getting too close to another man—the fear that such an interest in "brotherhood connections" could be misinterpreted as sexual. A straight Christian man in today's culture does not want to be perceived as gay or inadvertently send a message to another man that could be interpreted as sexual interest.

Shame

Shame over our sins, makes men want to hide, just like Adam and Eve did. It drives men into isolation. We easily feel like we are the only one with these struggles and fear rejection by the Christian community if anyone knew about them. This is especially true for Christian leaders who have the most to lose if their secret sins were exposed. Thus, men fear getting into deep relationships where there is accountability—even though in their heart, they know that such accountability could be the power they need to overcome their secret sins.

When Christian men are asked to identify their strongest temptations, lust is at the top of the list. They are especially ashamed of the dark side of their sexual fantasies, of masturbation, and of their struggles with pornography. They know that if some of their secret sexual thoughts were flashed on the PowerPoint screen at church for everyone, including their wives and daughters to see, they might run out of the church building and never come back.

Men also carry shame over past marriage failures, wayward children, their social or educational heritage, and their private struggles to overcome addictive patterns from past use of nicotine, alcohol, or other drugs. The body of Christ must create safe relationships within the fellowship where we can confess our sin, find strength in each other, and recognize that we are all in the process of being sanctified. But that is not happening as effectively as it should.

Too often we think of the church as a hotel for saints instead of a hospital for sinners. The corporate culture of the church easily becomes moralistic, subtly sending the message that this is the group that has it all together. The truth is the exact opposite; the name of our church should be "Sinners Anonymous."

Our fear of exposure is closely related to the next obstacle to male connection—our pride.

Male Pride

Our wives are certain that nearly all men came from the factory with a few computer chips missing, including the one that enables us to ask directions when we're lost. Although healthy self-confidence is a virtue, *self-reliance* can be a deadly form of pride. Self-reliance is what convinces men that they can earn their way into heaven. It is the form of human pride that sends people to hell—a refusal to acknowledge our inadequacy, our unfitness for an audience with a holy God, our need of a Savior.

In contrast, the core value of kingdom people is *dependence*. The first brush strokes of Jesus' portrait of his kingdom people given in Matt. 5-7 read, "Blessed are the poor in spirit, for theirs is the kingdom of God."

The Greek word, "poor" refers to those who are "spit upon," i.e. those on the lowest possible rung of society with no resources whatsoever. Jesus is teaching us that the highest virtue of his kingdom people is an attitude that daily recognizes our own utter spiritual poverty. When we come to the table to meet God, we bring ourselves plus nothing. Peter and James reinforce Jesus' emphasis on such poverty of spirit by reminding us, *"God opposes the proud, but gives grace to the humble."*[12] The foundational attitude for the Christian life is a humility that repudiates self-reliance and admits our fundamental *dependence* upon God and the others he brings into our lives.

Christian men need to realize that lurking in the dark places of the masculine heart is a proud resistance to admitting that we have to depend upon anyone else. *If we don't identify and confront that resistance, it will subtly steer us away from the connection with a band of brothers that we need.* It will cause us to lose sight of the covenantal nature of the Christian faith and the truth that we are not only called as individuals to be followers of Christ, but we are called into a community of Christ-followers.

The twin brother of self-reliance is *independence.* There is a virtuous independence that arises from our dignity as the image bearers of God, who are called to *rule for God* over His creation. The problem is that we are born with Adam's sinful nature. Adam wanted to rule *for himself.* Deep in our masculine soul is an overpowering desire to be independent, to rule autonomously, to be like God. We resist authority. We resist accountability. We resist restraint. We like the open road.

Unless you confront it head on, your sinful desire for autonomy will prevent you from connecting at a deep level with brothers in Christ. When the sharing level in a friendship or study starts to get personal you will find an excuse to stop meeting. Dwelling in our sinful hearts is a strong aversion to letting others get close enough to confront us, challenge us, or nag us about aspects of our lives that aren't right. We resist the tough accountability that would put an end to our self-indulgence, settling instead for mediocrity in our walk with Christ. Left unchallenged, our masculine resistance to accountability will rob us of the spiritual strength and personal fulfillment that come from connection to a band of brothers who love us and are helping us fight our spiritual battles.

Busyness

When most Christian men are asked why they don't have deeper friendships with a few Christian brothers, they answer, "I'm too busy." Nostalgically, they remember the days in college or the military when they had a couple of buddies they were close to. But, as men move into the "establishing" years of their lives, finding a mate, getting their career started, and beginning a family, they find that their new environment is no longer conducive to cultivating close male friendships. At the same time, their need for masculine friendship is masked because a new wife, buddies at work, and the arrival of children seem to meet their relational needs. Whatever opportunity they have to build relationships tends to be spent on superficial acquaintances, such as playing golf with a few guys from work or getting together with their families for a barbeque.

Because men are so task-driven, our conversation defaults to discussing the practical, visible, measurable world of business, news, politics, sports, the weather. We use the English language primarily to communicate the concrete facts and decisions that make up our world. (This is one reason we have so much difficulty communicating with our wives, who use words much more often to express emotion.) Men's tendency to default to superficial discussion is risky, however. Pat Morley warns:

> Like an iceberg, the beautiful part of our lives is that tenth
> or so which people can see. What's below the surface, how-
> ever, is where we live our real lives—lives often hidden
> from the scrutiny of other Christians. The jagged subsur-
> face edges of our secret lives often rip open our relation-
> ships and damage spiritual lives. What is unseen and not
> carefully examined can sink us when we are unaccountable
> for those areas of our lives.[13]

Unless Christian men are intentional about going beneath the surface and building a bond of brotherhood, they will naturally remain at the surface, cliché level in relationships.

A Faulty Church Model

Randy Pope, in his book, *INsourcing: Bringing Discipleship Back to the Local Church,* calls the church back to life-on-life discipleship. He writes, "If we look back over the course of recent church history, particularly here in the United States, it is apparent that somewhere along the way the church lost sight of the form of discipleship I am describing."[14]

Men are hardwired to respond to challenges. Consider what would happen if every man joining a church were given this challenge: *We believe that Christianity has always required BOTH a vertical commitment to walk with Christ in your everyday life and a horizontal life-on-life commitment to connection in the covenant community. You need to forge some brotherhood connections with a few guys you do life with.*

If the church leadership modeled this commitment and helped them in the process of building those friendships, *a lot more men would devote themselves to doing what is expected*, making it a priority to forge some brotherhood connections.

As it is, many good Christian men see having a best friend as a luxury. They would love to have a buddy to play golf with on Saturday mornings. But the truth is, they've put that pleasure on the altar as they exhaust themselves trying to be faithful to their responsibilities. Besides heavy demands on the job, they often have a family to manage, perhaps extended family to care for, a small group or church committee to lead, a Sunday School class to teach, families in the church to shepherd, and neighbors to reach out to with the gospel.

They are up to their eyeballs doing what men are expected to do in the church, which does not include connecting with a brother for encouragement and accountability. In their mind, making time to hang out with a best friend is an option that can wait until they are empty-nesters and retired. But, it must be asked, "From a biblical perspective, is having a brother to watch your back a luxury, or a necessity?" As you continue to read this book, you decide.

Blindness To The Spiritual Battle Around Them

A men's ministry leader said to me, "Gary, your analogy of needing a wingman is a great metaphor, and 'Got your back' is a popular way to say, 'I'm your friend.' But many Christian men don't really see the need for a brother to watch their back because most men don't think of their life as a spiritual battlefield."

I believe my friend is right. We church leaders have failed to show men that part of their fundamental identity as men is to be a warrior. In Genesis 2:15 we read, "The LORD God took the man and put him in the Garden of Eden to work it and keep it." The Hebrew word for "keep it" is *shamar,* which means "to guard," "to protect," "to watch over." Not only is Adam placed in the garden to *work it* by wielding the plow, but to *protect it* by bearing the sword. "Being God's deputy lord in the garden, Adam was not only to make it fruitful but to keep it safe."[15]

Adam failed in his responsibility to protect Eve from Satan's attack. The text makes it clear that he was standing right next to her during the temptation. Larry Crabb, in his book, *The Silence of Adam* proposes what perhaps Adam should have said.

> "Now wait just one minute here! Honey, this snake is up to no good. I can see right through his devilish cunning. He's deceiving you into thinking you have more to gain from disobeying God than by remaining faithful to him. That's a lie!
>
> "Let me tell you exactly what God said to me before he made you. And look around us. This is Paradise. God made it and gave it all to us. We have no reason to doubt his goodness....
>
> "Snake, this conversation is over. TAKE OFF!"[16]

Adam's decision to eat the fruit was "both an act of conscious rebellion against God, and a failure to carry out his divinely ordained responsibility to guard, or 'keep' (Gen 2:15) both the garden and the woman that God had created as a 'helper fit for him.'"[17]

God's design for manhood has always required us to fight spiritually by resisting temptation, and striving to shape our heart attitudes, marriages, homes, businesses, churches, and culture according to God's holiness. But as descendents of Adam we often seem to have inherited his passivity. John Eldrege recounts how his nine-year-old recognized that some men are absentee warriors.

Blaine came downstairs and without a word slipped a drawing he had made in front of me. It is a pencil sketch of an angel with broad shoulders and long hair; his wings are sweeping around him as if unfurled to reveal that he is holding a large two-handed sword like a Scottish claymore. He holds the blade upright, ready for action; his gaze is steady and fierce. Beneath the drawing are the words, written in the hand of a nine-year-old boy, "Every man is a warrior inside. *But the choice to fight is his own.*"[18]

As CS Lewis taught us, this world is enemy-occupied territory. To follow Christ is to enlist in his cause—the overthrow of Satan and establishment of Christ' kingdom of righteousness over every square inch of the planet. For his honor, we are to spread his rule spiritually to the very gates of hell and geographically to the uttermost corners of the earth. We are not on earth to accumulate material stuff but to strike a blow against evil. The man sitting on the sidelines in this fight, however, doesn't need anybody watching his back!

They Don't Know What They Are Missing

Asked if they have friends, nearly all men would say, "sure." Even guys with high privacy settings on Facebook have friends. Many guys receive tweets from friends and are on text message, and Instagram group lists. But they have no one to talk to when their boss infuriates them by dissing them in front of the other workers. They have no brother asking about their daily battle with lust or praying for their anger problem. No one is there to talk with if they found out their daughter was pregnant or their wife had threatened to leave them. In fact, they have no brother who even knows what their true spiritual battles are.

Few men have thought much about the differences between a superficial friend (whom we'll call an *acquaintance*), a good friend (whom we'll just call a *friend),* and a best friend (whom we'll call a *brother-in-arms.*) It is useful to consider these three general categories of friendship because it helps men see the kind of friend they are missing. Of course, these levels overlap, and some friendships seem to fit two categories. Yet, it is helpful to think clearly about the "exposure" levels of different relationships. The process of letting a friend get to know us can be compared to peeling off layers of an artichoke until its heart is revealed.

<u>Level 1: Acquaintance (superficial friend)</u>. An *acquaintance* is somebody we've allowed to get to know us on the surface by peeling off a few outer layers of information about ourselves. He or she is someone who friends us on Facebook, whom we decide to friend back. Acquaintances know our name, and are welcome to the surface information posted on our Timeline or About page—if we are in a relationship or not, where we work, who our other friends are, and other posts. Interaction is by definition, superficial in nature, and is usually related to pictures we post about our family members, our trips, our parties, or our accomplishments. The communication centers around the outer, visible world—whatever can be captured by the cameras on our phones. At this level it is usually unsafe to reveal much of what is going on in our soul. These are true friends, but the connection is superficial. Church dynamics experts say that the maximum number of people a person will know by name in the church is about fifty. In Jesus' life, this level may correspond to the seventy-two mentioned in Luke 10.

<u>Level 2: Friend. (good friend)</u>. An acquaintance becomes a *friend* when, after peeling off more layers, you discover common interests, opinions, likes and dislikes. Good friends are usually walking in the same direction. For example, you may share a common love for ultimate Frisbee, so your teammates become your friends. Perhaps one of your coworkers likes to work out like you do, so you begin heading to the gym together after work. In *The Four Loves*, CS Lewis observes that whereas lovers stand face to face absorbed in each other, friends stand side by side absorbed in a common interest. This is the depth of connection experienced by most couples' Bible studies. You begin to share your opinions, your values, your commitments. You may even begin to share general prayer requests. As the friendship deepens, some more layers of the artichoke come off easily and naturally.

In John 15:15, Jesus calls the twelve his *friends*. "No longer do I call you servants, for the servant does not know what his master is doing; but I have called you friends, for all that I have heard from my Father I have made known to you." Jesus uses the word, "friends" to describe the twelve, because he had taken them into his confidence. This level of friendship is very enjoyable, and most Christian men never go deeper. Consequently they remain alone in their spiritual battles. Few have considered that Jesus modeled a deeper level of masculine connection than friendship, a special bond with Peter, James, and John.

Level 3: Brother-in-arms (best friend). The most intimate events of Jesus' ministry were not shared with all twelve disciples, but only with Peter, James, and John who became Jesus' closest friends. Jesus peeled off more layers of the artichoke and allowed these "inner three" to know more of the core of his being. This deep level friend can be described as a *friend who sticks closer than a brother*, a *brother-in-arms*, a *brother who is in the battle with you*, a *best friend*. Men can experience this level of connection only with a trusted few who have grown close over time—for it is the result of inviting your brothers to know what is happening *in your soul*. It is a bond that is forged when you can be vulnerable enough and humble enough to begin to unzip your inner life and depend on your brothers to help you fight your moral, emotional, and spiritual battles. As deep support, love, and commitment grow, your band of brothers increasingly stands shoulder to shoulder with you, helping you fight your battles and watching your back.

This is a level of connection—a bond of brotherhood—that I believe all men long for. Yet, tragically, nineteen out of twenty Christian men don't experience it. *If they did, they would be able to point to a best friend*. But, the truth is that they have no one close enough to have their back.

Many such men are deluded about their true isolation. They may be in couples' Bible studies, adult Sunday school classes, or serve on church boards. They may experience a measure of comradeship on the church softball team, on the church board, or on the church's mission projects. But they have no brother with whom they are regularly and honestly sharing what is happening *in their soul*. And they don't know what they are missing.

The obstacles to forging a bond of brotherhood with some other Christian men are formidable. Bands of brothers do not arise out of thin air. *They only come about because a few Christian brothers are intentional about building them.* That is one of the lessons we will learn in the next chapter as we carefully examine the elements of the most famous friendship in the Bible, that of Jonathan and David.

Group Discussion Guide

1. Look back over the seven obstacles to male connection. Which two stand out most to you?
2. Did your growing-up years teach you to let others know what was going on inside or teach you to avoid letting others know what you are feeling and thinking?
3. Why do you think most men have trouble baring their souls to others?
4. How can Christian men overcome their sense of shame over their failures?
5. Is it fair or unfair to say that many Christian men are losing spiritual battles because they are too proud to recognize their need for a brother to fight beside them?
6. How would you respond to the statement, "Having a best friend is a luxury that I don't have time for at this stage of my life?"
7. Do you agree or disagree with the statement, "Unless Christian men are intentional about going beneath the surface and building a bond of brotherhood, they will naturally remain at the surface, cliché level in relationships?

During the week: Think and pray about this statement, "Bands of brothers do not arise out of thin air. They only come about because a few Christian brothers are intentional about building them."

Chapter 3

Jonathan and David

"YOUR LOVE TO ME was more wonderful than the love of a woman." What words are these? Perverted words? Twisted words? The words of some pathetic sexual deviate?

No. A war-hardened veteran penned these words after his best buddy fell in battle. They were written by a warrior, with the piercing grief only a soldier mourning for a comrade-in-arms could begin to understand.

Twisted words? No. They are words straight and true—a swift, clean arrow shot from the heart of Scripture. David wrote these words after the death of his friend Jonathan on the bloody slopes of Mount Gilboa. What the son of Jesse expressed without shame in that lament was something that has burned deep in the soul of every man in one way or another for generations beyond memory. A desire for friendship, man to man. A desire for friendship with nothing between. A yearning for friendship so real, so strong, so compelling, it is willing to share everything about itself and make deep and powerful promises.

Down deep at the core, every man needs a friend. Down deep at the core, every man needs a brother to lock arms with. Down deep at the core, every man needs a soul mate.[19]

No doubt, our wives are to be our most intimate companions. And, it is for our wives and children that we are to pour out sacrificial love. We are called to die *for* them. But, as Stu Weber points out, "something inside us longs for someone to die *with*…someone to die *beside*…someone to lock step with. Another man with a heart like our own."[20] Jonathan found that kind of brother in David. The elements of this famous friendship constitute many of the elements that make up the *Check 6* partnerships discussed in chapters 8-10, which men around the country are building.

Souls Knit Together

In 1 Samuel 18:1, after Jonathan witnessed David's victory over Goliath, Scripture tells us that his soul was "knit together" with David's. A look back at the fourteenth chapter explains why. There, Jonathan attacks the Philistines and wins a great victory for Israel that is quite similar to David's victory over Goliath.

Like David, Jonathan could not stand the passivity of the Israelite army. Like David, he understood that the battle was the LORD's, saying to his armor-bearer, "Come, let's go over to the outposts of those uncircumcised fellows. Perhaps the LORD will act in our behalf. Nothing can hinder the LORD from saving, whether by many or by few." Like David, he courageously faced an overwhelming Philistine force. Like David, he prevailed against enormous odds, killing some twenty men with the help of just his armor-bearer. Like David, his victory caused the entire Philistine army to be routed.

In short, Jonathan and David were kindred spirits, warriors who were jealous for God's honor, willing to take the battle to his enemies, depending upon his power for victory. They are an inspiring pair of comrades-in-arms, whose earthly battles are an Old Testament picture of the invisible, spiritual battles Christian men are called to fight.

Jonathan Loved David as Himself

In Romans 12:10, Paul commands Christians, "Love one another with brotherly affection. Outdo one another in showing honor." There is no clearer Biblical picture of such love than Prince Jonathan's love for a shepherd boy named David.

In 1 Samuel 18:1 we read that Jonathan loved David *as himself.* To love someone "as yourself" means to be as committed to meeting his needs as you are to your own. Practically speaking, that means when your brother has a need, you drop what you are doing and go.

Jim and Bill were best friends who enlisted together to fight in World War I. During the long muddy days of trench warfare in Europe, the battle became a stalemate. Every so often the men would be ordered over the top to move up to the next trench; but in this new era of the machine gun, row upon row would be mowed down.

On one particular occasion, Jim and Bill were ordered over the top to advance to the next trench. Enemy fire broke out and Jim fell mortally wounded. Bill worked his way back in retreat to the previous trench with his commanding officer. He could hear Jim out on the battlefield crying, and wanted to go rescue him. But his commanding officer said, "No, don't risk your life. Didn't you see where he was hit? He's a gonner." But when the C.O. turned away, Bill went out of the trench into the fire to be with his friend, Jim.

A little bit later, he returned alone to the trench in a hail of bullets. The C.O. snapped, "Why did you do that? I told you he wasn't going to make it. He's dead isn't he?"

Bill said, "Yeah, he is."

The C.O. replied, "That was the stupidest thing you could have ever done."

Bill mumbled, "But he was alive when I got there."

"He was—well what did he say to you?"

Bill answered, "He said, 'I knew you'd come…I knew you'd come.'"[21]

Such brotherly love was on display in our congregation one morning when Clint rushed his wife, who had a sudden, unexpected heart attack, to the hospital. As soon as their pastor called them, Clint's closest brothers went to the hospital, where they found that she had died. The brothers canceled their work commitments and remained with him until relatives arrived. Before leaving, they decided among themselves what each would do what in the coming weeks and months to be there for Clint.

Someday every one of us is going to have to face a major crisis in our lives. What are the names of the brothers who will help you walk through it, when it happens to you? Are you part of a band of brothers like Clint was?

Back in the text, Jonathan's love for David went even beyond loving him *as himself*. Verse four of 1 Samuel 18:4 reads, "Jonathan took off the robe he was wearing and gave it to David, along with his tunic, and even his sword, his bow and his belt." What a picture of fulfilling Paul's later admonition, "In humility count others more significant than yourselves."[22] Jonathan was royalty; David was a peasant and as a shepherd, one of the lowliest at that. Furthermore, there was every reason for Prince Jonathan to see David as a rival and threat, just as his father, Saul, did. After all, Jonathan was not only the crown prince, but a great warrior like David in his own right.

But he overcame his masculine rivalry, stripped himself of the royal robe he wore to put it on David, also giving David his royal sword and bow. The gift of his sword was especially striking, since the Philistines had removed nearly all the swords from Israel so that they could not be used in a revolt. Jonathan was willing to step aside and make way for his friend. Several chapters later, he even says to David, "You will be king over Israel, and I will be next to you." (I Sam. 23:17)

Such honor is a critical part of masculine relationships. Men operate in a tough, competitive work world and without realizing it often bring a subtle spirit of competition into male groups. For a band of brothers to be effective, its members must be committed to honoring each other above themselves. Praising each other's strengths and celebrating each others' successes is a vital way to keep male rivalry from hindering brotherly love.

Jonathan Formed a Covenant with David

During my growing up years, I had a best friend named Dave Myers with whom I built a tree house. We only had three of the four trees we needed, so we went out into the woods, cut down a tree and sank it in cement as our fourth pillar. My father had been in the storm window business, so we used some old undersized sample windows and a four foot storm door to give it a little class. After we finished the construction, we celebrated by spending the night in it. That evening, we decided to take out our pocket knives, slit our fingers, and mingle the blood. We became blood brothers.

27

Little is known about the nature of Jonathan's covenant with David, except that David honored it by always welcoming Jonathan's descendants to his table, when he became king. The one thing we *do* know, however, is that as in my friendship with Dave Myers, Jonathan and David wanted to be *intentional* about their commitment to each other as friends. *The intentionality reflected in the cutting of a covenant marks one of the most distinctive characteristics of men's groups that makes those men become true brothers-in-arms.* The first step down the path that goes from being just a group of friends to becoming *brothers-in-arms* is the intentionality of going deeper. It is a decision to single out a brother or several with whom you *intend* to build a bond of brotherhood.

Another component of covenants is that they are based upon promises made to each other *which provide the commitment needed in order for the relationship to thrive*. This is easily seen in the marriage covenant. In marriage, husband and wife are able to more safely bare their bodies and souls to one another because of the covenantal vows they made to love each other unconditionally. In front of God, the church, the state, their parents, and friends they have vowed to love one another till death. These vows provide the security that allows them to be naked and unashamed.

There is a principle here that is worth noting when it comes to exposing our souls in order to form a bond of brotherhood. Baring our souls is not healthy without certain protections that keep us from being harmed by our vulnerability. When I was a sophomore at Penn State, I participated in a twenty-four hour T-Group through the psychology department. This was a group of total strangers with no agenda for the twenty-four hours except to open up to one another. I later realized that this experience was like having a psychological one night stand. I was expected to bare my soul for this one night to those who had made no commitment to care for me one bit after those twenty-four hours were over. Such vulnerability under such circumstances is fundamentally unhealthy.

For a band of brothers to experience an environment in which soul issues are shared and prayed over, several protections are indispensable. The most important is confidentiality. Whatever is shared with each other must remain with those brothers alone, unless it is illegal or severe enough for the church leadership to be involved. The men participating in men's groups may have strong marriages in which husband and wife always share everything. That will have to change or they cannot be a part of the band of brothers. The problem with group members being able to share a confidence with just one other person is that soon the whole world knows what happened. Ben Franklin seems to have understood human nature when he said, "Three people can keep a secret as long as two of them are dead." Lack of iron-clad confidentiality will kill a men's group. Men cannot bare their souls if they think some man's wife in the group may hear all about it.

Besides confidentiality, another protection that a band of brothers must have is *time for trust to grow*. No healthy person bares his soul in front of strangers. There must be enough time for the commitment level, the vulnerability level of other members and the trust level to grow. Among healthy men, the ability to bare their souls is directly proportional to the trust level in the group. That is why when we re-designed the *Check 6* questions in chapter 8, we decided to let each man choose his own accountability question. During the early formation of the *Check 6* partnership, every man should pick a "safe" accountability question that he will not be too ashamed to answer honestly.

Jonathan Had David's Back

When Saul told Jonathan of his intent to kill David, Jonathan went to David and warned him, "My father Saul is looking for a chance to kill you. Be on your guard tomorrow morning; go into hiding and stay there. I will go out and stand with my father in the field where you are. I'll speak to him about you and will tell you what I find out." (I Sam. 19:2-3) Later, he fervently interceded with his father, arguing vehemently on David's behalf.

Jonathan, like any good soldier, understood the importance of watching his blood-brother's back. He saw David's susceptibility to being attacked by his father, and took action. In the military, "I've got your six" is all about protecting your brother's back, which is his point of greatest *vulnerability*. A fighter pilot needs a wingman watching his six o'clock because he is most vulnerable to being shot down from behind. An Army Ranger needs a battle buddy watching his back for the same reason.

When it comes to spiritual warfare, having a brother who has my back means that he knows my places of *spiritual vulnerability*. I have exposed those points of weakness to him and asked for his help in those battles. For him to "have my back" in these skirmishes, he has to regularly ask me about them. This process is what we call *accountability*. When I want a brother watching my back in some area of temptation, it means not only giving him the right to ask about that spiritual battle any place, any time—*it is requesting him to do so*.

I realize that when "accountability" is not rooted in grace, or when it is used harshly, rather than tenderly, it becomes legalistic and destructive. Nevertheless it must be said that you really don't have a brother watching your back if he does not have permission to ask you regularly about specific spiritual battles in your life. Unlike two army battle-buddies who can physically see threats to each other's backs, we can't see the spiritual attacks on our brother. The only way to watch his back spiritually is to regularly ask about his spiritual successes and failures.

Despite the bad reputation that accountability has, it is also worth noting that most Christian men want more accountability. Sr. Pastor, Don Sampson of Crossroads Church, Woodbridge, VA conducted a professionally designed survey of the men in his congregation. The survey asked a series of questions about five areas of discipleship: knowledge, equipping, accountability, mission focus, and prayer. The men were asked to evaluate in what ways the church was providing for their needs in each of those five areas. By far the biggest gap between the perceived need of the men and what Crossroads was providing was in the area of accountability. Sampson writes, "The level of desire for accountability among the men of Crossroads and the perceived lack thereof is very significant, even startling. Our plan for men's discipleship must address this gap."

Tom Joyce, the Men's Pastor at Immanuel Bible Church in Springfield, VA expects every one of his men to meet with at least one other man for prayer, encouragement and accountability. Tom saw the power of accountability—even among unbelievers—while serving as a squadron commander in the US Navy, shortly after the Navy Tailhook scandal took place. This scandal refers to a series of incidents in which U.S. Navy and U. S. Marine Corps aviation officers were alleged to have sexually assaulted numerous female coworkers. Tom writes:

> The predominant number of guys who got involved in
> the Tailhook scandal were from the West Coast F14

community. So I was hand-selected to go to this squadron since the commanding officer and executive officer had both been relieved of their duties because of their involvement in things surrounding Tailhook.

Before we left for that deployment, we got all of the families together in the movie theater at the air station there. We told the families how much we loved their guys. I said, "To the best of our ability, I will bring every one of these guys home and all of our airplanes and we will do the mission of the country." Then we left for deployment.

As soon as I had opportunity, because we were going into our first port visit, I got all my guys together—thirty-six officers—in the Ready Room. I said, "I know what the background of this squadron has been. You've lost a CO and XO because of that. But things have changed. Here's what I'm going to do. We're heading into a port visit tomorrow, and if it comes to my attention that any one of you men has done anything immoral behind your wife, or girlfriend's back, I'm going to send you home. I don't care where we are on the deployment, I'm going to send you home and one, you will pay your own way home, and two, you can knock on the door and explain to your wife or girlfriends why you came home."

You could have heard a pin drop in that room. The meeting ended. One young lieutenant came up to me and asked, "Permission to speak frankly, Sir?"

I said, "Sure"

He said, "You're an idiot" (I wasn't expecting that much frankness!) He continued, "You can't dictate your morals on us. You can't tell us what we can and can't do on our own free time in port."

I told him, "Number one, adultery is a violation of the Uniform Military Code of Justice. It's against the law. Number two. Go ahead and push me. You'll be the first to go."

For the next few weeks it was difficult. But we got into a combat zone and operations spiked up. I was leading these guys over the beach and crazy things like that. Everything got back to normal—just as a fighter squadron should be—a really, really close- knit group of guys.

We came home six months later on December 23rd. As I said I would, I brought every one of those men and planes home. In fact I led a ten-plane formation over the flight-line of Miramar Naval Air Station, thousands of family members and friends waiting for us to come in. As the CO, I landed first. So, as each pilot took his flight gear off, I went up, shook his hand, and I said, "On behalf of a grateful nation, I welcome you back to the United States. Thanks so much for your great work and encouragement to me following my leadership. Now go see your family and Merry Christmas to you."

Everyone of these guys—they didn't want to say it publically—but nearly every one of these men would shake my hand, grab me close, and say, "Thanks for holding me accountable. Thanks for helping me do the right thing."[23]

Not all of Tom's flyers believed it at first. But as his officers had headed into port for some R & R, he still had their back. And when they got home to their girlfriends and families, they were glad he did.

In today's world, every Christian man needs a band of brothers who will help him fight his spiritual battles and have his back. Jonathan was that kind of brother to David. Some have speculated that if Jonathan had not died in battle, David's affair with Bathsheba would have never happened. Jonathan would have had his friend's back. He would have been in David's face about taking more than one wife and about staying back at the palace while the troops were out in the field. With Jonathan's kindred zeal for God's glory, it is likely that their friendship would have strengthened David, making him less vulnerable to his lust. We'll never know. But we do know that Jonathan had David's back. As warriors battling Satan, the world, and our sinful nature, we need someone watching our six, just as David did.

What an attractive picture—having a brother with whom you share a deep bond, your souls knit together by a common loyalty to the High

King of Heaven, a common passion for his honor, and a common willingness to fight for his cause. Wouldn't you love to have a brother who constantly builds you up, celebrates your successes, and is there for you when you need him? Wouldn't it be great to know there is someone in your corner who labors tirelessly to help you in your spiritual battles, never shaming you, but keeping a vigilant eye on your back? We're proving across America that such a bond is *not* merely some idealized fiction. It can become a reality. As we will see in the next chapter, it is the kind of relationship which our Lord wants his followers to have.

Group Discussion Guide

1. What stood out to you the most about Jonathan and David's friendship?
2. What do you think of Stu Weber's statement, "something inside us longs for someone to die with…someone to die beside…someone to lock step with. Another man with a heart like our own?"
    Have you ever had a friend like that?
3. How did Jonathan demonstrate Paul's later command, "Honor one another above yourselves?"
    How do you think those actions affected the natural rivalry we could have expected between Jonathan and David?
4. Has the word, "accountability" held a mostly positive or mostly negative connotation for you in the past? What is the relationship between having another brother's back and accountability?

Over the next six weeks, we will be adding one of the six questions that are part of the *Check 6 Partnership* system presented in more detail in chapter eight. Please answer these "Checks."

<u>Check #1</u>: What encouragements or successes have you had this past week?

During the week: Think and pray about what elements of Jonathan and David's friendship you would most like to have with a few brothers.

Chapter 4

Jesus' Teaching and Example

Rising to his feet, Bob struggled to speak through his tears, "I want to confess to you brothers that I need help with my Internet pornography problem. I've only been married two years. I thought marriage would fix the problem. But it hasn't."

Slowly Sam stood to his feet, "Brothers, I too have a major problem with pornography, and I know it is wrong."

Next, Bill stood up but kept looking at the floor, "I am having the same problem."

Then Brian got up and said, "Several years ago, even though I was a full-time leader of a ministry, my struggles with pornography nearly destroyed my marriage and ministry. I'd like to offer to start getting together with you guys—and others in the room who are struggling with this problem—for study, prayer, and loving accountability. This is not the kind of battle you can win alone."

That was the way the weekend retreat I led on sexual purity ended. These brothers realized that they could not fight their battle for sexual purity alone; so they made the commitment to connect with a few other brothers. Brian's words echoed in my mind, *"This is not the kind of battle you can win alone."*

Christian men are called to engage in a fierce spiritual battle with sin; and too many of them are alone in their struggle. Lone Ranger

Christianity, however, is not Christianity at all. It is an aberration. Our Lord's call to follow him *has always required connection to others in the body of Christ*.

This fact is clear when we consider Jesus' call to the twelve to follow him. The greenhouse, which Jesus chose for growing his disciples, was the context of male friendship. He called twelve disciples to "be with him," which also meant being with each other. The twelve learned *together*, served *together*, lived *together*, at times failed *together*, and eventually faced growing hostility *together*.

Jesus' discipleship approach was NOT meeting with Peter on Monday morning for breakfast, setting aside Monday lunch for Andrew, then meeting John for breakfast on Tuesdays, etc. *His discipleship approach was to form a band of brothers who were with him as he lived his life*. If the church has any hope of strengthening its men, it must get men into relationships with other men. It cannot continue to largely ignore the need men have for connection.

If Jesus' relationship with his disciples teaches us anything it shows that being a disciple of Jesus Christ requires BOTH a vertical commitment to surrender to Jesus Christ AND a horizontal commitment to connection with others in the body. This is irrefutable; yet many men think they can succeed at being Christ's disciples when functionally they are not a part of a band of brothers! The result is that their outward commitment to Christ looks great, while inwardly they are often losing battles with temptation, allowing their hearts to be captured by the world's idols, struggling in their marriages, and caring very little for the lost, whom Jesus came to seek and to save.

Jesus further underscores this principle of male connection in the way he sent his disciples out to minister. Mark records, "And he called the twelve and began to send them out two by two, and gave them authority over the unclean spirits. He charged them to take nothing for their journey except a staff—no bread, no bag, no money in their belts— but to wear sandals and not put on two tunics." (Mark 6:7-8) You DON'T need a cooler full of food, a duffel bag with your personal items, extra money, or even an extra change of clothes. But there is one thing you DO need. YOU DO NEED A BROTHER.

In Luke 10:1 Jesus sends out the seventy two, and once again it is two by two. "After this the Lord appointed seventy-two others and sent them on ahead of him, two by two, into every town and place where he himself was about to go". Perhaps the reason Jesus sent them out in pairs is seen in verses 17-19 where he makes it clear that their ministry was spiritual warfare.

In case his followers were still confused about the horizontal connection that is fundamental to Christ-followers, Jesus underscores relational connection when he gives his church its marching orders, in the Great Commission.

> *Go therefore and make disciples of all nations, baptizing them in the name of the Father and of the Son and of the Holy Spirit, teaching them to observe all that I have commanded you. And behold, I am with you always, to the end of the age.* (Matt. 28:19-20)

In verse nineteen Jesus assigns the church the goal that is to be its single focus, making disciples. In verse twenty, he gives two vital clues for *how* disciples are made. The first is *baptizing them....* Whether one holds to believer-only baptism or infant baptism, in both cases baptism is a sign and seal of membership in the covenant community. Jesus reminds his followers right in the midst of giving the great commission, that being his follower is not just about a vertical relationship to him but *always includes a horizontal connection to the covenant community.*

As verse twenty continues, Jesus reveals a second clue about how disciples are made: *teaching them to observe all that I have commanded you.* Jesus' emphasis on daily obedience is consistent with the common understanding of *discipleship* in his day. A "disciple" (*mathetes*) was the follower of a master who patterned his life after the life of the master. The master's *disciples* were a group of like-minded followers who did life together. So at the core of Jesus' Great Commission is the concept that his followers are to apply his teaching to their everyday lives....*together.*

Not only does Jesus' approach to discipleship require his followers to be relationally connected, so does our Lord's example. As mentioned earlier, our Lord forges a *bond of brotherhood* with Peter, James, and John that goes well beyond his relationship with the other disciples.

There are three significant occasions in Jesus' life when he asked only these three close friends to join him. These glimpses into Jesus' life provide clues we can use to form a picture of the *bond of brother-hood* he experienced as a man. Since Jesus' divinity is so important to our theology, we sometimes forget that he was also fully man. Through his human nature he modeled ideal manhood—a manhood that reveals *not isolation* but *connection with other brothers*. Let's consider the three occasions to which Jesus invited only Peter, James and John.

1. The Healing of Jairus' Daughter

It seems that from the beginning of his public ministry, Jesus was intentional about strengthening his close relationship with his inner circle. Early in his ministry, he was called to the bedside of the twelve year old daughter of Jairus. (Mark 5:37-42) He permitted only three of his followers to go with him to the daughter's bedside, *Peter, James, and John*. The setting was a private one—bereaved parents gathered around the bed of their deceased daughter—in contrast to Jesus' other healings which were almost all public. The intimate tenderness of the scene is captured by Mark's repetition of Jesus' exact words in Aramaic, "Talitha koum" which means, "Little girl, I say to you get up!" Whatever his reason, Jesus chose to allowed only the inner three to experience his intimate interaction with the family and his extraordinary miracle.

Of course the inclusion of just Peter, James, and John in this incident can be over-emphasized. After all, the girl's bedroom was probably much too small to accommodate the twelve—but then Jesus could have made all his disciples wait outside while he alone and experienced these intimate moments with the girl and her family alone.

Maybe Jesus wanted the future writers of Scripture to witness this event. After all, Peter would write two epistles, and also give eye-witness testimony to Mark for his gospel. And John would write his gospel and three epistles. However, if this were Jesus' reasoning, then why wasn't Matthew invited into the bedroom and why was James (the son of Zebedee, who is not the James who wrote the Epistle of James) not included? The best interpretation of the facts is that Jesus had a deeper friendship with Peter, James, and John and invited only them to witness his intimate interaction with Jairus' family. As we think about the growth of friendship it is worth noting that as a friendship deepens we invite that friend more and more into our *other relationships*.

The subsurface part of our lives, the part men keep nicely protected below the waterline, involves our *relationships* with others. Inviting another brother into the private world of that relationship builds a bond with him. I discovered this truth in my relationship with my friend Ken. I was with him as he held his wife the moment that she died. I put my arm around him and wept with him. As I listened to his anguish poured out to God, I knew it was a sacred moment; I was peering into his very soul. It was a high privilege to be with Ken during these most intimate moments with his wife, and God. Those sacred moments together created a bond between us that will never be broken.

A friendship moves towards a bond of brotherhood when two or more men trust each other enough to share honestly what is going on in their soul — *and much of that soul activity has to do with our closest relationships*. A man may share some troubling doubts he has been having in his relationship with God or perhaps his son's problem with pornography. He may open up about the problems he is having in his marriage, or the painful feelings of rejection he feels from his father. He may decide to risk being honest about his daughter's drug problem or the troubling details of his poor performance rating at work. In doing so, he is peeling off a few more layers of the artichoke — letting the brothers know a bit more about him *because they are hearing about his relationships with others*. He is taking the courageous steps required to go from a mere friendship to a deeper bond of brotherhood.

2. The Mount of Transfiguration

In Mark 9:2ff, Jesus takes only Peter, James, and John with him up the mountain where he is transfigured before them. The other disciples are not allowed to see his glory revealed. John would later write, "The word became flesh and dwelt with us. We have seen his glory, the glory of the One and Only who came from the Father, full of grace and truth," (John 1:14.) It was only to his most intimate friends, Peter, James, and John that Jesus gave this momentary, unique revelation of his true identity. Obviously, more is going on here than deepening his friendship with the inner three. The glory of Jesus' divine nature is revealed, a unique event in redemptive history. Nevertheless, Jesus also modeled a second characteristic of a bond of brotherhood. *He lifted the shade to let his closest brothers see more of his true identity.*

When you forge a bond of brotherhood with other men, you begin to let them see you *as you really are.* For sinful creatures like us it means that you stop putting up a front. You stop trying to impress others with your spirituality. You stop pretending you are fine *when you really aren't fine.* You begin to take down the masks. You begin to let others see your weakness and sin. Only when the masks are down can authentic connection between brothers take place.

3. The Garden of Gethsemane

As Jesus faced the cross on the night before he died, he did not go out into the wilderness alone to pray, as he had so often. He did not go alone to battle Satan, as he had at the beginning of his ministry. This time, he took his closest brothers with him.

> *And they went to a place called Gethsemane. And he said to his disciples, "Sit here while I pray." And he took with him Peter and James and John, and began to be greatly distressed and troubled. And he said to them, "My soul is very sorrowful, even to death. Remain here and watch." And going a little farther, he fell on the ground and prayed that, if it were possible, the hour might pass from him. And he said, "Abba, Father, all things are possible for you. Remove this cup from me. Yet not what I will, but what you will." And he came and found them sleeping, and he said to Peter, "Simon, are you asleep? Could you not watch one hour? Watch and pray that you may not enter into temptation. The spirit indeed is willing, but the flesh is weak."* (Mark 14:32-38)

On this night of agonizing wrestling with the Father's will, an internal trauma so excruciating that he sweated blood, Jesus was intentional in having his closest brothers with him. He'd brought the twelve to the garden, but only took his closest friends, Peter, James, and John further with him. He then revealed to the inner three the heart-wrenching struggle of his soul. "My soul is sorrowful even to death."

He asked them to watch *with him.* And even though he walked a few yards away from them to pray by himself, he repeatedly came back to them! In fact, Jesus was distressed that they were too sleepy to join the battle with him. In Jesus' unselfish love for them, he was probably thinking of their temptation more than his own. But he still wanted them to be with him in his hour of greatest travail. The strongest spiritual warrior who ever lived—the prototype of masculinity—wanted his closest brothers with him as he stared the ordeal of the cross in the face.

The third level of sharing modeled by Jesus with his inner core of friends is to *stand with each other as you face your spiritual battles.* Men who have forged a true bond of brotherhood with a few other men don't have to fight their battles alone. Such brothers stand shoulder-to-shoulder, fighting together and for one another. When one is too weary to lift his shield of faith, the other brothers fight for him even more fiercely. They surround him with words of encouragement. They agonize for him on their knees in prayer. They search the Scriptures for insight that might help their brother. They encourage him through a quick text message or email, or call him to see how he is doing. He is not alone in his struggle!

That is the fundamental difference between a mere friendship with a Christian man and a *bond of brotherhood.* Friends don't know what is going on beneath the surface, inside your soul. They don't know what you are struggling with, so how can they know how to help? How can they fight in prayer for you? How can they encourage you? How can they be in your corner? Your friends who don't know your spiritual battles can't help you. You are stuck fighting your battles alone.

If our Lord, the perfect model of true manhood, forged a bond of brotherhood with a few close friends, ought not we to do the same? If he wanted his closest brothers with him in the garden as he faced the most severe trial of his life, isn't it logical that we also need brothers to stand shoulder to shoulder with us in our struggles?

In the next chapter we will see that the depth of connection expected of Christ-followers by the New Testament writers is astounding. Could it be that in this Western culture, that idolizes independence and autonomy, we have missed what Scripture really teaches about the depth of the brotherhood bond God wants Christian men to enjoy?

Group Discussion Guide

1. Why do you think Jesus called his disciples to be part of a band of brothers?
2. Why do you think Jesus sent the twelve and seventy-two out two by two? How does this apply to us?
3. Do you think most Christians today believe that being a follower of Christ means <u>both</u> a vertical commitment to Christ and a horizontal commitment to some brothers?
4. In what ways is it harder for Christian men today to become a band of brothers than it was for Jesus' band of twelve?
5. What stood out to you about Jesus' relationship with his closest friends, Peter, James, and John?

<u>Check #1</u>: What encouragements or successes have you had this past week?

Note. Jesus asked Peter, James, and John to pray for him as he fought his most severe spiritual battle. The last of the *Check 6* questions allows you to share a spiritual battle that you are comfortable sharing, so your brothers can pray for you. You might want to record each brother's request to support him during the week.

<u>Check #6</u>: What spiritual battles can I help you fight through my prayer for you?

During the Week: Pray specifically to support each other in your spiritual battles.

Chapter 5

The Biblical Case Against Isolation

"Your son, Christian, has been arrested for narcotics possession. He's in jail, but we'll have him out on bail in a few hours." These were the words coming over the phone line to Chuck Colson from his attorney while he was in prison.

Colson continues the story, "I couldn't reply; my stomach went again, like someone had kicked me in the middle. I thought I had been through all the tribulations one person could take. My son in prison seemed the worst blow of all...

The brothers at Fellowship house rallied to my aid. On Tuesday, January 28, Al Quie called. "Chuck, I've been thinking about what else we can do to help you. All of us today signed a letter to the President appealing for mercy, but is there anything else?" The voice on the other end didn't sound like Al; the words came slowly and seemed laden with sadness.

"Al, you guys are doing everything possible," I told him, "and I love you for it. I just don't know what else you can do."

"There's got to be something else, Chuck. I have been thinking." There was a long pause. "There's an old statute someone told me about. *I'm going to ask the President if I can serve the rest of your term for you.*"

Stunned, I could only stammer a protest. Al Quie with twenty years in Congress, was the sixth ranking Republican in the House....That very day, Doug Coe sent me a handwritten note. All the brothers would volunteer to serve my sentence, he explained.[24]

*C*huck Colson was getting a taste of the brotherhood bond that I believe God wants all Christian men to experience. It was through this brotherhood that Chuck Colson was discipled.

The Commands in Hebrews 10

And let us consider how to stir up one another to love and good works, not neglecting to meet together, as is the habit of some, but encouraging one another, and all the more as you see the Day drawing near. (Heb. 10:24-26a)

This prohibition against Lone Ranger Christianity could not be clearer. Simply stated, these verses are a command to be connected to other believers. The message of the New Testament is that we need each other. We can't make it in the Christian life alone. This message is implied in all three exhortations:

1. Consider how to stir one another up
2. Don't forsake meeting with one another
3. Encourage one another

You cannot *consider how to stir a brother up* to do a better job of following Christ if you have no idea where he thinks he is failing. How can you "consider how to motivate him" if you aren't close enough to him to know where he is fired up and where he is dragging. Not only that, but the Greek word *stir up* implies a close enough connection that you have the right to *irritate* your brother, which is what the word "stir up" really means. The only other place this Greek word is used in the New Testament is to describe the "sharp disagreement" which Paul had with Barnabas in Acts 15:39 over John Mark. So, Hebrews 10:23 is best translated, *"Irritate one another to love and good deeds."*

What seems to be in view are the kinds of relationships where the right to challenge each other and to be frank has been earned, where over time, the trust and commitment level has grown to the point where love means speaking the truth. What comes to my mind are the kinds of masculine relationships where men say to each other, "How's your thought life been lately?" or, "Brother, maybe I'm wrong, but it seems to me that you're rationalizing," or, "Bob, I know you've been busy, but frankly you've been *saying* that you're going to have that heart to heart talk with your son for a month. When are you going to *do* it?"

What is in view in this verse seems to be the occasional pointed statement you sometimes have to make to a brother because you're committed to helping him face the truth about a situation. Such frankness is not usually part of a mere friendship, but is much more in keeping with the *bond of brotherhood* Jesus wants us to have with a few men.

Next, in Hebrews 10, believers are commanded *not to forsake meeting with other believers*. In context this command cannot be satisfied simply by showing up at church. The first century believers met in house churches, where they broke bread and experienced *koinonia*—the sharing of their lives with one another. (Acts 2:42) In context, *not assembling together* means not being in a relationship with other believers where there can be *stirring one another to love and good deeds* (vs. 24) and the *encouraging of one another* (later in vs. 25). The call to believers in this verse is to shun isolation and get connected to the body. That is a call that twenty-first century Christian men need to hear! Is it a call you have fully obeyed?

The third exhortation, like the first, requires close relational connection to be put into action. You cannot *regularly encourage someone* who never reveals what is going on in his soul. Unless he lets you know what is going on in the subsurface part of his iceberg, you have no way of knowing he is discouraged. This text makes it absolutely clear that God does not want any Christian to go through life alone in his battles. He wants each of us to have deep enough connections to other believers that we are continually encouraging one another. The superficial friendships that most Christian men have don't enable the encouragement God commands.

Members of Each Other

Certainly this call to connection is obvious in Paul's teaching on the body of Christ. In Romans 12:5 he writes: "So we who are many are one body in Christ, and individually *members of one another*." Gene Getz, in his book, *Building Up One Another,* explains:

> The New Testament clearly and unequivocally states that Christians are members of one another. All New Testament authors recognize this truth. But it was Paul who developed the concept extensively in his correspondence with certain churches. It was Paul who exclusively used a unique illustration to get his point across—the human body. In his letters… he penned the word 'body' (*soma*) more than thirty times to illustrate the functioning church.[25]

Going it alone, as most Christian men are doing, is a daily denial of our very identity as followers of Christ. We should be daily redeemed *out of* our sinful autonomy, proud independence and consequent isolation, and *into* the community of the redeemed—a family in which we are connected as members of one another. Connection to other believers is part of the definition of being a Christian. In fact, Jesus said it is this very connection that identifies us in the world. *"By this all people will know that you are my disciples, if you have love for one another"* (John 13:35).

It is overwhelmingly clear from the New Testament "one another" commands that *going it alone* is inconsistent with our identity in Christ. Christians are commanded to:

Love one another with brotherly affection (Rom. 12:10).
Love one another earnestly from a pure heart (1 Pet. 1:22).
Outdo one another in showing honor (Rom. 12:10).
Build one another up (1 Thess. 5:11).
Live in harmony with one another (Rom. 15:5).
Teaching and admonishing one another (Col 3:16).
Serve one another. (Gal. 5:13).
Bear one another's burdens (Gal. 6:2).

Encourage one another (1 Thess. 5:11).
Confess your sins to one another (James 5:16).

These commands cannot be obeyed, apart from a relational connection with other members of the body that goes far beyond superficial friendship.

The Covenant Community is God's Ordained Environment for Spiritual Growth

The concept of individuals becoming isolated, disconnected followers of Jesus Christ is foreign to Scripture. A Christian, by definition, believes in Christ and becomes a member of the community of faith, which is called the *covenant community*. Indeed, that membership in the covenant community is what both of the church's sacraments are about. Baptism is a sign and seal of membership in the Covenant of Grace. It is a sign that sets apart those who are baptized, marking them as properly belonging to the covenant community. The Sacrament of the Lord's Supper, often called Communion, signifies our union with Christ *and with each other*. By definition, being a Christian means being connected to others in the covenant community. *This connection goes vastly beyond having your name on the church membership roll or sitting in church Sunday morning.*

God does not intend for any believer to experience the trials of life *alone*. He has ordained that his people be a part of a community where, "If one member suffers all the members suffer with it, if one member is honored all the members rejoice with it" (I Cor. 12:26). More and more Christian counselors are recognizing that their clients are best helped through the counselee's involvement in Christian community. God has designed us so that his process of restoring our soul, after we have been wounded, cannot happen in isolation. We need someone outside ourselves to listen to our experience and to understand our pain before we can respond to it as God would have us do. A few Christians who gather together for close connection, where the trust level has grown and there is a willingness to be vulnerable, is what Larry Crabb calls *the safest place on earth*. This is where people connect and are forever changed. He writes,

47

> We need each other never more than when we are most broken…A central task of community is to create a place that is safe enough for the walls to be torn down, safe enough for each of us to own and reveal our brokenness. Only then can the power of connecting do its job. Only then can community be used of God to restore souls.[26]

It should not surprise us that Christian psychologists recognize the need for relational connection to help those dealing with issues of the soul, since everything about this universe reflects the relational nature of God himself. *Even God doesn't go it alone.* God exists as a relationship; we call it the Trinity, and God's relational fingerprints are all over the universe. No aspect of life works when we are alone. Paul commands the Ephesians to put off the old self and put on the new self which is in "the likeness of God." The proud *old self* lies to us that we can be self-reliant. It makes us fear vulnerability. It resists accountability, desiring instead to continue indulging in sinful pleasures. The *new self* is the opposite. It is not isolated, autonomous, or independent. Rather, it reflects the nature of God—a *relational connection to other members of the body*. Such connection requires more than sitting beside someone in a Sunday school class or worship service.

Despite the strength of the biblical argument against isolation, it may take years for this message to sink into the heart of a man. It may not be until he reaches mid-life that he begins to realize that he has not invested enough in the important relationships of his life. But by then, a lot of damage has already been done. In the next chapter, we will consider what it costs Christian men when they don't get around to implementing God's command in Hebrews 10:23 to be connected to others in the Body of Christ.

Group Discussion Guide

1. Read Heb. 10:23-26. What have you learned over the years about how to encourage other believers?
   What do you think of this statement: "You cannot regularly encourage someone who never reveals what is going on in his soul?"
2. Look back to the list of "one another" commands. Which of these commands simply imply special treatment of believers that we barely know, and which ones require us to have more than a superficial relationship with other believers?
3. How is "going it alone" inconsistent with our identity in Christ?

Check #1: What encouragements or successes have you had this past week?

Since Christ-followers are trying to pattern their lives after the example of their master, Jesus, and obey his commands, many have tried to establish the daily habit of reading a Bible passage and praying. *Check 6* Partnerships, without being legalistic, try to reinforce this habit by asking each brother to share something from the Word (his own reading, a sermon, or audio). Discussing how to apply Jesus' teaching to life is what disciples do. Here is the Check #2 question.

Check #2: What biblical insight or verse from your quiet time has stood out recently?

Check #6: What spiritual battles can I help you fight through my prayer for you?

During the week: Pray for the spiritual battles of the men in your group.

Chapter 6

The High Price of Isolation

I have formed the habit of asking about accountability when stories of someone's spiritual defection or moral fall come to my attention. Without fail, I ask something like, "Was _____ accountable to anyone on a regular basis? Did he (or she) meet with one, two, or three folks for the purpose of giving and receiving counsel, prayer, and planning?" Without exception—*hear me, now*—without a single exception, the answer has been the same. "NO!"[27]

The Cost to Ourselves

Over the years I've observed that when we Christian men cease to be connected to other Christian men for encouragement, support, and accountability, we begin to display most of the following characteristics.

1. We become undisciplined. Without the encouragement and accountability of other brothers, laziness and self-indulgence continually undermine our consistency. We easily become undisciplined in eating, exercise, getting up to have time with God, praying for family members, and controlling our temper, tongue, and eyes. Pat Morley writes,

Some men have spectacular failures where in a moment of passion they abruptly burst into flames, crash and

burn. But the more common way men get into trouble
evolves from hundreds of tiny decisions—decisions
which go undetected—that slowly, like water tapping on
a rock, wear down a man's character. Not blatantly or
precipitously, but subtly, over time, we get caught in a
web of cutting corners and compromise, self-deceit and
wrong thinking which goes unchallenged by anyone in
our lives.[28]

2. We become tired. Iron sharpens iron; sticks rubbed together pro-
duce heat. Our passion is stimulated, and our motivation is rekindled
through close friendship. That stimulation energizes us as we head out
into the world to face heavy responsibilities.

Without such connections to replenish us, our spiritual energy dissi-
pates. The inner fires that fuel our motivation begin to cool, like a burning
log that is taken out of the campfire. When that happens, all our responsibilities seem heavier. One Christian businessman laments,

> I'm tired, blessed, but *alone*. In one year, we've seen a
> ten-fold increase in business, and that's exciting. But, I'm
> tired because I feel alone. Yes, I have a wife who is very
> supportive; but there are no men supporting me. When I
> read in Exodus 17 of Moses being lifted up by other men,
> I watch a TEAM of men fight the Amalekites, the hated
> enemies of the Israelites. Moses gets tired and yet Aaron
> and Hur, his two friends hold him up. God, I need some
> Aarons and Hurs in my life to join me.[29]

He describes the condition of countless Christian men: *tired. Tired* from
the daily battle; *tired* in the midst of success; *tired* because we have no
team of men to join us in our struggle; and *tired* because when our arms
grow weary, we have no close brothers to hold us up.

3. Our blind spots cause us damage. Every day, Christian men fail
morally, relationally, spiritually, and financially—not because they set
out to fail, not because they don't work very hard, but because of their

blind spots. Without another set of eyes to help them see, men can make decisions that set them back decades or cost them their families, their fortunes, and their careers. Robert Lewis, of Men's Fraternity observes, "One of the significant downsides of isolation for a man is that he ends up with a warped perspective on life. One of the worst things a man can do is to only deliberate with himself because it is so easy for him to lose perspective and reach the wrong conclusion."[30]

Proverbs 15:22 teaches, "Plans fail for lack of counsel, but with many advisors they succeed." Proverbs 24:6 instructs, "for waging war you need guidance, and for victory many advisors." Without friends who are close enough to have their finger on our pulse, we are bound to make some bad decisions. Poor is the man who has no friends close enough to challenge him. "Wounds from a friend can be trusted, but an enemy multiplies kisses" (Prov. 27:6). We need brothers who will speak the truth to us, help us recover perspective, and point out our blind spots.

4. We lose sight of our priorities. No man gets a yearend bonus or a vacation to Hawaii for being patient with his wife or being a great dad. The world doesn't reward us for following Christ's priorities. To the contrary, the pursuit of other priorities sometimes pays visible short term dividends. The intoxicating, workplace rewards of recognition, respect, power and money will keep a good number of us motivated well past quitting time.

Christian men need the constant reinforcement of our brothers for living out the values of Christ's Kingdom, which contrast so sharply with the world's values. We need to hear, "well done," from Christian brothers, because the world isn't going to pat us on the back for our obedience to Christ.

We should not underestimate the need of our masculine hearts to hear words of affirmation. One morning my four-year-old son, Tim, got up before the rest of the family and went down to the kitchen. He dragged a chair over to the cabinet and got down six cereal bowls along with all the cereal we needed. He then completely set the table for breakfast. When I came down to the kitchen and saw what he had done, I said, "Tim that is wonderful! You have just shown a very important character quality called 'initiative,' which is *recognizing and doing what needs to be done before you are asked to do it.*"

He couldn't even pronounce the word. "Yeah, initiatitif." When each of the other kids came down I raved to them about Tim's taking the initiative. Guess what happened in our kitchen before breakfast the next two days! The table was already set! Affirmation has tremendous power to keep us motivated. *Without brothers in Christ pulling for us to keep our priorities straight, we start listening too much for the world's affirmation, becoming shaped by its values.*

5. We become more susceptible to secret sins. Without accountability, it is much more difficult to resist temptation. Private lusts, visits to pornographic web sites, illicit relationships, and other secret sins have the opportunity to flourish. Without accountability, we get away with our rationalizations and excuses to move into compromise because there is no one to challenge them.

Our unwillingness to make ourselves accountable to others gives us permission to continue in these private sins. Joe Dallas, an instructor of the *Every Man's Battle* workshops warns,

> Sexual sin thrives in the dark. If you're caught up in any sexual vice, one thing is certain: the secrecy surrounding your behavior is what strengthens its hold on you. However ashamed you may feel about admitting your problem to another person, the reality is this: *You can't overcome this on your own.* If you could, wouldn't you have done so by now?[31]

One of the eight core kingdom values revealed to us by our king is given in Matt. 5:6: "Blessed are those who hunger and thirst for righteousness, for they shall be filled." A true hunger and thirst for righteousness will drive men to recognize their need for other brothers to pray for them in their battles and to hold them accountable for their behavior.

6. We become comfortable with mediocrity. "As iron sharpens iron, so one man sharpens another" (Prov. 27:17). Without the sharpening we need from soul contact with other men, our spiritual lives become dull: missing worship happens more often, making a financial sacrifice for a ministry becomes less frequent, talk radio may replace time listening to a Christian speaker or extra time praying in the car, special time set apart for the LORD gets crowded out, we give up trying to find time to pray together with our wives. In short, our passion to seek first the kingdom of God is no longer stirred by gathering with brothers to share what God is doing in our souls. *Without that stimulus, spiritual passion cools*.

We may also accept the status quo in our marriage. With all that we have on our plate, it is easy to treat our wives the same way we treat our cars: *We take them for granted until there is a problem*. Such an approach is a far cry from loving them with the sacrificial love modeled for us by Christ. But, without brothers to inspire and encourage us to keep dying to self in order to put our wife's needs ahead of our own, we lose sight of Christ's command to husbands. The demands of work, the complexity of our relationship with our wives, and busyness on the home-front conspire to move this primary command for husbands to the back burner.

In a similar way men who are not connected to other men at a deep level can easily find themselves lowering the bar when it comes to discipling their kids. The home front can be very discouraging. We know that we have enormous influence in the lives of our children through our relationship with them and through fervent intercessory prayer on their behalf. Yet, without brothers to keep us on track, we can easily squander the enormous potential we have to build into their lives. Instead, we can settle into a passive mediocrity when it comes to our role as dads. So long as the kids are reasonably obedient to us, go to the youth group, aren't getting too many D's or F's, and aren't into drinking, sex, or drugs, we feel like there is nothing to do. But, if we are to be obedient to the command to "raise up our kids in the way they should go," we need other brothers pushing us to disciple our kids and to keep the home front a priority.

Without other brothers pushing me, I also find that my commitment to reaching out to others with mercy or the gospel begins to wane. Without brothers stimulating us, encouraging us, and inspiring us by their example, it is easy to withdraw into our Christian castle and pull up the draw bridge. We stop confronting our cold-hearted lack of concern for those whose lives are broken by sin. We stop pushing ourselves out of our comfort zone to build relationships with unbelievers. We stop being burdened to care for the destitute, for whom life is not working.

We stop being concerned about our unfaithfulness in sharing our faith with the lost.

Take a moment and be brutally honest with yourself. Is your life showing some of the characteristics of a lowered bar? Is it possible God is leading you to see the need for some brothers in your life to stoke your passion for Christ and his kingdom?

Cost to Those We Love

The sad reality is that spiritual flabbiness doesn't just hurt *us*; it damages *those we love most*. The first casualty is God's reputation. Instead of honoring our Lord by representing him well, our spiritual dullness, worldly values, and surrender to temptation bring shame on his name. He's the most wonderful being in the universe. How can we not love him more? How can our loyalty to him not be fiercer?

Spiritual mediocrity also hurts our families. I become less sensitive to my wife's needs, less likely to be on my knees for her, and more inclined to wound her with lousy attitudes and sharp words, making it more difficult for her to respect me. When my abiding relationship with Christ, the vine, suffers, the quality of spiritual fruit in my life goes down, which is sorely felt by my family. I become more selfish and less loving, angrier and less patient, more indulgent and less self-disciplined.

The cost of our spiritual weakness doesn't stop there, however. God makes it clear that our impact on our children goes even to several generations beyond them. It goes beyond our families as well. Weak men make for weak families. Weak families make for weak churches. Weak churches lose their impact as salt and light in the nation. The present, weak condition of Christian men has brought our nation to the point of crisis. In the words of James Dobson,

> The western world stands at a great crossroads in its history. It is my opinion that our very survival as a people will depend upon the presence or absence of masculine leadership in millions of homes.... I believe, with everything within me, that husbands hold the keys to the preservation of the family.[32]

The price tag for the isolation of twenty-first century Christian men is enormous. But across the nation, more and more Christian men are rising up and saying, "ENOUGH! I refuse to let *mediocrity* be the defining word for my Christian life. I *need* to be connected to a brother for encouragement and strength." The next chapters tell the stories of how churches are building men's discipleship ministries that help men connected below the waterline and of individual men across the country who are manning-up to forge the brotherhood connections God wants them to have.

Group Discussion Guide

1. Look back over the six characteristics displayed by Christian men who are not connected to other Christian men for encouragement and accountability. Which of these characteristics concern you the most? Why?
2. What stood out to you about the cost to those we love when we are not connected to other Christian men?

This week, we add Check #3 to our discussion questions. *Check 6* brothers want to support each other in their family leadership responsibilities

Check #3: What has been the most difficult part of being the spiritual leader lately?

Note: Single guys can skip Check #3 or use the question to talk about their relationship with someone they are currently dating, with room-mates, or with immediate family.

Check #1: What encouragements or successes have you had this past week?

Check #2: What Biblical insight or verse from your quiet time has stood out to you recently?

Check #6: What spiritual battles can I help you fight through my prayer for you?

During the week: Pray for the spiritual battles of the men in your group

Chapter 7

Rediscovering How Disciples Are Made

The reason men get into trouble isn't so much that they don't understand what they are supposed to do, but rather that they have no structure to help give them the discipline to do that which they already know they should.

Recently I asked a group of men about the frequency of their golf game. The few who said they played regularly also said they have a standing game—structure. Among the majority who didn't play regularly, no one had a standing game.

If we are going to beat the "old man" in each of us, we are going to have to organize to do it. The only men who are consistently having accountable relationships have planned and committed themselves to a specific structure or program—they have a "standing game." Our accountability "checkups" need to have the priority and consistency of a weekly allergy shot.[33]

The brotherhood connection men need is not random; it requires intentionality. It requires *getting organized to beat the old man*. But how do we do that? Might the New Testament teaching on discipleship provide clues about the *structure* men need to give them the discipline to do what they know they should? Let's investigate.

The Early Church

The year was 62 AD. The imprisoned church planter was spending hours interceding for the numerous churches he had planted around the Mediterranean. Several years earlier, he had completed his greatest theological tome, The Letter to the Romans, in which he had said very little about the church. Now, in the closing years of his ministry, he turned his thoughts to the functioning of the body of Christ. He picked up his quill to explain to the Ephesians that the church is the bride of Christ, who is its Head. Shortly afterwards he penned his letters to Timothy and Titus, all of which were focused heavily on how the church was to function.

Paul knew that Jesus had given the church one central mission, *to make disciples*. It was obvious *how Jesus* had made disciples of the twelve. A master with his band of disciples was a common sight in Paul's day. Jesus had called the twelve to follow him as their master—to be with him, to follow his teaching, to pattern their lives after his, to become a band of brothers. For three years, he was their mentor, training them to be his apostles.

But after Jesus' death and resurrection, what was to be the discipleship pattern in the church? After all, three thousand had come to faith after Peter's sermon on the Day of Pentecost, which grew to five thousand men alone shortly afterwards.[34] If mentoring were the New Testament discipleship model, each of the twelve would have had to start to mentor over four hundred men!

What was Jesus' plan to make disciples, now that he is no longer physically present on earth? Paul's answer was spelled out in his letter to the church at Ephesus. Christ, the Head continues to grow his followers through one particular mechanism: *the proper functioning of his body, the church*. Paul's teaching in Ephesians and the Pastoral Epistles could be summarized by saying that disciples are made as the church functions both as an *organization* and as an *organism*.

In Paul's letter to the Ephesians, we see both of these functions. He writes, "And he gave the apostles, the prophets, the evangelists, the shepherds and teachers to equip the saints for the work of ministry for building up (discipling) the body of Christ" (4:11). He gives the job description of the leaders of the church as an *organization*. It is to equip the rest of the members of the body to accomplish their job. But when Paul explains what every congregational member's job is, he uses the analogy of the human body—the church functioning as *organism*.

Let's further explore these two concepts of church as *organization* and church as *organism*. In Paul's teaching, the church has a clear hierarchical structure, which fits an organizational flow chart. At the top is Christ, the Head of the church. Right below him is the board of elders (sometimes called pastors, bishops, or deacons) This board, called the "session" in my communion, exercises the very authority of Christ in the oversight of church discipline, the teaching of the Word, and the administration of the sacraments. The elders are also commanded by Peter to be under-shepherds for the Chief Shepherd: "Shepherd the flock of God which is under your care" (1 Pet 5:1). This *organization's* purpose is to grow fully mature disciples up into Christ, the Head.

Paul's letter to Titus shows his concern for the church to function as *organization*, with qualified leaders overseeing it. He writes, "This is why I left you in Crete, so that you might put what remained in order and appoint elders in every town as I directed you…" (Titus 1:5). I smile at the expression "put what remained in order." My denomination, the Presbyterian Church In America, and the churches in its Reformed heritage are famous for doing things *decently and in order*.

But, for disciples to fully grow up into Christ, the church's engine must be fully firing not just on the cylinder labeled *"organization"* but also on the cylinder marked "organism." A few verses later in Ephesians 4, Paul employs the metaphor of the physical body, stressing that believers must *be connected to one another*.

> *Rather, speaking the truth in love, we are to grow up into him who is the head, into Christ from whom the whole body, joined and held together by every joint with which it is equipped, when each part is working properly, makes the body grow so that it builds itself up in love.* (Eph 4:15-16)

Notice the rather odd structure of this sentence. Paul is saying that the body of Christ is built up (equipped) through… *the joint*. The body is equipped with *joints*. The joint is the *connecting point*—the place where two members of the body come together. The only way a Christ-follower can grow up into maturity as Christ's disciple is to be *connected* in the body of Christ. **Disciples are made not through programs but in relationship**. Jesus' discipleship methodology, since his ascension, is for his followers *to disciple one another.*

The discipleship process in the twenty-first century still requires talking with other Christ-followers about obeying Jesus' teaching in their everyday lives, just as Peter, James, and John talked about following Jesus as they walked the dusty paths of Palestine. But today, Jesus' teaching comes from his Word (Scripture) instead of from his lips. The discipler is still Jesus—not through his physical body but through the members of his body, the church.

The need in the twenty-first century church, then, is not for more disciplers—we are all supposed to be disciplers of each other! **The need is for better connection**—intentional bonds to be built where Christ-followers are *speaking the truth in love*. That is Christ's plan to build up his disciples to maturity. For twenty-first century men, it means *forging a bond of brotherhood* with a few men for encouragement and accountability.

After spending the past ten years helping churches around the country more effectively disciple men, I've come to this conclusion. When a church is not functioning well as an *organism*, i.e. its members have not connected in speak-the-truth-in-love small groups, there is enormous pressure on the exhausted pastors and elders to provide, through their shepherding, all the relational support that members need. The problem is that church leaders *cannot provide the majority of the relational connection believers require*. That has never been Christ's plan. Believers must be connected in the body. *They must be functioning effectively as an organism.*

Tom Joyce, a retired Navy pilot who had been stationed at Naval Air Station Miramar, gives us a great picture of the church functioning as organism. He recounts:

> Six other brothers and I met in the chaplain's office every Tuesday morning at 6 AM for Bible study and prayer. These were strong brothers—accountability partners of mine.

61

"They found out that I had been selected to command a squadron that was located right down the road from the chaplain's office. One Tuesday morning, they all got to the study early, but when I arrived there was a note on the door, 'Report to Squadron 111 immediately.' That was the squadron I was going to command.

So I drove over to the squadron, a young sailor let me in and took me upstairs to the commanding officer's office, and there were my six brothers in that office. They had a chair in the middle of the office and said, 'Here's your chair.' They sat me down and one spokesman of the guys said, 'We know you're heading to this squadron right here to be the CO in the next couple of months. We want to help prepare you for that.'"

Then, one by one, they began praying into me the leadership principles from Joshua 1. 'Will you help this man, God, to know your word?' 'Will you help this man, God, to live out your word?' 'Will you help this man, God, to never forget who he has to report to—that he reports to you?'"

You see, I had 270 men, an all-male fighter squadron, thirteen airplanes each worth fifty-five million dollars, and umpteen number of families connected to these men—a huge responsibility on my shoulders. And I knew where I was going. I was taking these men to a combat zone. My brothers sitting here with me were helping to prepare me for leadership.[35]

The body of Christ was functioning as *organism*.

A Zoom Lens Look at Ephesians 4:15-16

Let's dig further into verses 15 and 16 of Ephesians, where Paul gives us amazing insight into Jesus' present methodology for making disciples. Observe that in verse 16, Paul says three times that every single member of Christ's body must be *connected* to the other members. I have bolded these in the text.

> *Rather, speaking the truth in love, we are to grow up into him who is the head, into Christ from whom the **whole body**, joined and held together by **every joint** with which it is equipped, when **each part** is working properly, makes the body grow so that it builds itself up in love.*

Notice in verse 15 that Paul does not assume that our spiritual growth is automatic, even though it is Christ who causes the body to grow. He exhorts us to grow up into Christ the Head: "Rather.... we are to grow up into the head."

In the middle of this exhortation, Paul reveals exactly how this building up process works: *by speaking the truth in love*. Here are the three indispensable parts of this disciple-making process:

1. Speaking. Consider the action required in the discipleship process. The verb is not "reading," although reading Christian books is a great way to grow spiritually. Paul doesn't say, "listening to great sermons," even though being fed the Word is foundational for spiritual growth. The action Paul commands is not "imitating older Christians," or "reading your Bible," or "attending church," though these are great ways to grow in Christ. The action required for this process is startling; it is *speaking*.

According to this verse, every single member of the body of Christ must have some connection to other believers in his church life that is small enough so that he is regularly verbalizing, talking, *speaking*. This requirement for discipleship to take place has huge implications. No matter how biblical the preaching or inspiring the Sunday morning worship, congregational members' spiritual growth will be stunted unless they are connected in groups *small enough for each member to speak*. As we have seen throughout this book, the vast majority of Christian men have no such connection. No wonder so many Gallup and Barna polls show very little difference between the way Christians and non-Christians live! They are not in God's ordained discipleship process.

2. The truth. As verse 15 continues, Paul tells us what each member of the body of Christ is to be speaking *about*. In context, Paul uses the word *truth* in contrast to being "carried about by every wind of doctrine" (verse 14), so we know that he is referring here to the Word of God. How the Word of God applies to everyday life is to be the topic of discussion by which the body "builds itself up."

This teaching is thoroughly consistent with the basic concept of discipleship. A disciple follows the example and teaching of the master. By definition, Christian discipleship is about obeying Jesus. He said, "If you love me, keep my commandments" (John 14:15), and "If you abide in my word you are truly my disciples, and you will know the truth and the truth will set you free" (John 8:31-32). Discipleship in Jesus' mind was about abiding in the truth of his teaching.

However, there is also a secondary meaning implied in Paul's word choice. The Greek verb for "speaking the truth" used here comes from *a,* which means, "not," combined with the verb for, "hide" *lanthano*. So it means *not concealed* or *not hidden*. Dietrich Bonhoeffer observes that real fellowship cannot happen when believers cover up their struggles with sin.

> It may be that Christians, notwithstanding corporate worship, common prayer, and all their fellowship in service, may still be left to their loneliness. The final breakthrough to fellowship does not occur, because, though they have fellowship with one another as believers and as devout people, they do not have fellowship *as the undevout*, as sinners. The pious fellowship permits no one to be a sinner. So everybody must conceal his sin from himself and from the fellowship. We dare not be sinners. Many Christians are unthinkably horrified when a real sinner is suddenly discovered among the righteous. So we remain alone with our sin, living in lies and hypocrisy. The fact is that we *are* sinners![36]

Being honest with one another, instead of hiding our struggle with sin is Paul's point in this text. If all I ever share with a brother is my success, I am probably building thicker walls (of self-protection) around myself. In contrast, to share my failure is to build a bridge between us.

The first two steps of this disciple-making process, then, can be summarized as *speaking honestly with a few believers about how you are succeeding and failing to apply Christ's teaching in your life*. Admittedly, this summary may seem a bit contrived—even formulaic. That is because it is! Paul is giving us a formula for how disciples are made. *If discipleship is our goal* the only agenda that makes disciples is to honestly discuss the intersection of God's truth with our lives.

This book is to some degree rooted in the belief that there is a creation-need that men have to bond with other men. The camaraderie of team sports, serving together in the military, hanging out with buds at the sports bar for a beer, or even meeting for a Saturday morning church breakfast reveal this basic longing for male friendship. Nevertheless, male friendships among Christians do not take us down the path to spiritual growth *unless there is a vulnerable willingness to talk about our own struggles to obey what scripture teaches*, i.e. speaking the truth to one another...

3. In love. The "truth-speaking" connection within the body of Christ, that every believer needs to grow to spiritual maturity, is a bond defined by the word *love*. In these two verses, Paul not only says that our truth speaking is to be *in love* (vs 15) but that the whole process of building up each other is done *in love* (vs 16).

The bond of connection described by Paul is a real, personal, organic relationship, where there is love. Since "truth-speaking" connections in the body are our Lord's means for discipling his followers, church leaders naturally want to help their members build such connections. This is such an important goal that we will devote chapter ten to it. But it is worth noting that there is an important balance to be maintained in helping these relationships materialize.

On the one hand, there is a place for intentionality and structure—challenging men to forge relationships with one another where their agenda is sharing their spiritual battles, perhaps including a covenant by which they agree to pray for each other and keep what is shared confidential. But on the other hand, there is a subjective, organic side to a real friendship in which love for one another grows. Overly structured, forced, or mechanical connections will likely remain superficial and fail to grow mature disciples.

Some years ago, I was returning home after speaking at a men's retreat. My flight was delayed, leading to an unusually long layover at the airport. Emotionally empty and bored I walked into the airport book store, where the words, "erotica" beamed across the room at me. Being the godly man that I am, I took a step towards the bookshelf, rationalizing that I would probably make love to my wife when I got home and this might spice up our love life. However, as I took the next step, a little voice inside said, "If you look at that, you are going to have to tell Mark." Mark was a brother I had requested to ask me if I had looked at anything inappropriate on the trip.

As I took another step towards the erotica shelf, I responded to myself, "I can lie to Mark."

After my next thought, however, a light bulb came on inside. The thought was "I don't want to lie to Mark. I value our relationship too much." I suddenly realized that accountability doesn't work in superficial relationships. We men will just deceive our "accountability partner" one way or another. The kind of relationships that we have called *Check 6 Partnerships*, the kind described by Paul in Ephesians 4:15-16, are not superficial "accountability partners" a man is assigned by church leadership or coerced into having after his wife discovers his porn habit. Rather, they are relationships in which a deep commitment to each other has grown over time, a commitment that means that though I am not crazy about confessing my shameful failures to my brother, in the end, I will choose that path over lying to him every time.

This kind of loving, truth-speaking connection must be balanced between *being structured*—meeting together regularly with the application of scripture as our agenda, and *being organic*—a real friendship that can't be programmed, in which love and closeness grows. On the one hand we *make* this relationship happen by being intentional. Yet on the other hand we *let* such relationships happen, because they are natural, organic, real friendships. This balance is vital.

As we have helped hundreds of men across the country build these truth-speaking friendships (forge bonds of brotherhood), we have observed that this friendship becomes the arena in which the members of this partnership live out many of the one-another commands of Scripture: be devoted to one another, fervently love one another from the heart, admonish one another, bear one another's burdens, confess your sins to one another, etc. They are speaking the truth to one another *in love*.

This connection is also a primary arena in which spiritual gifts are exercised. It is in this small band of brothers that a man with the gift of serving hears about a practical need he can meet. It is in a small group, in which every member speaks, that one with the gift of encouragement discovers that a brother is down and considers how he can lift up that brother's spirit. It is hearing a friend describe the pain of his suffering that enables one with the gift of mercy to apply the salve of Christ's compassion to his wound. The body of Christ is being Christ to each other—building itself up in love.

To summarize, in the twenty-first century, since Jesus, the master, is no longer here in bodily form to mentor his disciples, it needs to be asked, "How is the risen Christ continuing to make disciples?" The answer is through a concrete process—*every believer in relational connections small enough that we can talk about how to apply scripture in our everyday lives, forming a bond of love.*

If this is what Paul believed about how disciples are made, we might expect to see some example of this pattern in the early church. And in fact, that is exactly what we see. Dr. Luke's description of the house meetings of the early church reads, "And they devoted themselves to the Apostle's teaching, and to fellowship (*koinwnia*, which means "the sharing of life"), to the breaking of bread, and to prayer" (Acts 2:42 NIV). Though there appears to be some gathering of the Jerusalem Christians in the temple courts, their core meeting structure was not a gathering in a lecture hall to listen to the senior pastor preach to thousands; it was to meet in house churches, connections small enough for each member of the body to be *speaking the truth in love.*

When Paul tells us in Eph 4:15-16 that disciples are made through life-on-life connections, his words make sense for two reasons. First, it is completely consistent with what we've seen in the prior chapters of this book—that Jesus has always called his followers to both a vertical commitment to Him, and to a horizontal commitment to connection in his body.

The second reason Paul's *speak-the-truth-in-love* methodology rings true is that it is consistent with what we've already observed about discipleship in our own experience. Although the structure or format may differ, we've noticed that when believers get together to talk about how to apply Scripture in their everyday lives, spiritual growth takes place. It may be the small groups on a men's or women's retreat, couple's home groups, table discussions after a Men's Fraternity meeting, a Navigator staff member meeting for Bible study with a guy for breakfast, a Samson Society or Celebrate Recovery support group meeting. A brief glance around the Christian landscape verifies this truth—that when these three elements are present, 1) everyone speaking, 2) conversation centered on honest scripture application, and 3) a growing bond of love is forming—discipleship is happening.

Discipleship In Different Life Stages

Despite the clarity of what Paul teaches in Ephesians 4 about how the church is to grow disciples, enormous confusion in the church surrounds the term *discipleship*. To some, the command to make disciples of all nations is the call to evangelize. To others, discipleship is a basic training course for new Christians. Others will argue vehemently that discipleship is about mentoring and multiplying: The pastor should disciple two elders who in turn disciple two men who will in turn disciple two more men, etc.

Is there some lens we can put over this discussion that can bring discipleship into better focus? I believe there is. We need to consider discipleship through the lens of the **various life stages** of a believer.

Consider the example of the three different life stages of an army recruit. He attends *basic training*, moves to his battle station where he is part of a *combat unit*, but may end up in a *field hospital* if he is severely wounded. The US Army's help for the soldier is different in each of these categories.

Boot Camp	Combat Unit	Field Hospital
Need basic training	Need battle buddy	Need Support/Recovery

These same categories make a useful paradigm for understanding one who enlists to become a disciple of Christ. As an infant believer, he needs structure, content, and **basic training** at spiritual **boot camp** from a mentor. Here, he receives training in the basic doctrines and disciplines of the Christian life.

But, unless he is uniquely called as an instructor, he doesn't remain at boot camp year after year. He graduates to take his place as an adult member of the body of Christ and to live out his commitment to Christ in everyday life. This stage of his spiritual life corresponds to his battle station in the army, where he is part of a **combat unit**. His need in this life stage is a spiritual **battle buddy** watching his back, someone to help him with his spiritual battles, a relationship connecting him to the body of Christ. His focus changes to collegial (mutual) discipleship, as a spiritual adult.

In a fallen world, however, where believers still experience the brokenness of sin, a Christ-follower may need specialized care and assistance for the severely wounded—a spiritual **field hospital. Support** and **recovery** groups, which are specially designed for those seeking to break their slavery to alcohol, pornography, drugs, gambling, etc., have a necessary place in our thinking about discipleship.

These three life stages of discipleship change lives because all three fit the life-on-life discipleship process given by Paul in Eph. 4:15-16, *speaking the truth in love*. Let's drill down a bit more to examine specific ministries designed to match these three categories of discipleship relationships.

Spiritual Boot Camp

The Navigators are renowned for their effective disciple-making. Few people realize, however, that Dawson Trotman, the founder of the Navigators, made a vow to the Lord to share the gospel with someone every day of his life. The result was that he constantly had so many new Christians around him that he had to design transferable materials to disciple them. His band of men who had just finished his discipleship curriculum were needed to turn around and help mentor another batch of new Christians. Also, the men and women in his ministry who needed to be discipled were mostly in the apprenticeship stage in life, in the military or in college. Mentoring is especially valuable at this stage of life. So the Navigator's discipleship model was a mentoring/multiplication model from the beginning.

The world-wide success of the Navigators' mentoring multiplication approach to discipleship is undeniable. The Navigators' ministry has gotten millions of men connected with other men, and women with women, life-on-life, talking about how to apply scripture in their everyday lives, and building a bond of love. Because their discipleship approach follows Eph. 4:15-16, their discipleship impact in the past has been staggering, and I believe the Navs will continue that impact into the future.

Journey Groups, a more recent and church-based ministry begun by Randy Pope, will continue to build disciples because Journey Groups follow the *speaking the truth to one another in love* methodology of Eph. 4 as well. Randy explains these groups:

> Journey Groups are 6-8 people who meet weekly for life-on-life missional discipleship. Each member signs a one year contract committing to the group. But the journey— the groups and the curriculum—can last up to three years, with some members rotating in or out each year....Most groups go long and deep into the Word, into what it means to live obediently and missionally, and into prayer.[37]

Journey groups are gender specific, which allows a much deeper connection than couples' home groups. They successfully get believers *speaking the truth to one another in love*. In addition, their exceptional curriculum and focus on outreach make them a highly valuable tool for the church to use in its calling to train disciples. The success of Journey Groups in making disciples, like that of the Navigators, is undeniable.

However, we must be careful not to let the success of our spiritual boot camp training program lead us to the conclusion that it is the normative discipleship methodology of the New Testament. Our methods for discipling *spiritually adult* believers need to be different from our methods for discipling *young believers*, **as surely as a father needs to treat his son differently when he is** *twenty-five* **than he did when he was** *five*.

Combat Unit

Once a believer reaches spiritual adulthood, the discipleship model is *mutual* discipleship. It still needs to be life-on-life, a speak-the-truth-in-love connection; but the relationship is collegial rather than hierarchical.

Let's return to the spiritual life stage analogy. Suppose a man I'll call Jack comes to faith in Christ at age twenty and is immediately invited into a discipleship group with a three-year curriculum. Because this group is an ideal tool for basic training in discipleship, Jack grows spiritually like a weed. After completing the three-year curriculum, he signs up again and completes another three years, this time as an assistant leader.

Now Jack is twenty-six. Assuming Jack lives to be seventy, what should be the discipleship plan for the next forty-four years of Jack's life to help him to continue to grow up into Christ? Often, those using excellent basic training materials on the topic of discipleship have a *one size fits all* answer—become a leader, using the same discipleship materials. But Jack, like the majority of Christians, does not believe he has mentoring gifts. He is not called to be a spiritual boot camp instructor.

May I suggest that the answer for Jack to continue spiritual growth the next forty-four years is to move from spiritual **boot camp** to a spiritual **combat unit**? He needs the same life-on-life connection that he has experienced in his earlier discipleship training group. But he needs to be a part of a combat team—where the focus is less on learning and more on fighting. He is no longer in the boot camp training stage of the Christian life. He has moved on in the spiritual life cycle to *adulthood*. He needs to be part of a band of brothers doing life together, who watch each other's back.

How a man can build this kind of brotherhood connection is so important that the next three chapters are devoted to it. But, before moving on, there is one other phase of the spiritual life-stage that deserves our attention.

Field Hospital

Sometimes disciples, like soldiers, endure severe wounds. In the same way that a wounded warrior sometimes needs a field hospital to recover and get back on his feet, Christ-followers sometimes have a special need for support and assistance as they recover from life-impacting wounds.

As the church moves into the twenty-first century there has been a welcome rise in church-led, Christ-centered support groups. Such groups bind their members together through the shared pain and mutual struggle of facing job loss, divorce, serious illness, sexual addiction, the death of a loved one, substance abuse, etc. It is worth noting that when such groups maintain a biblical focus, they fit Paul's description of the discipleship process—*speaking the truth to one another in love*. And such groups can provide enormous spiritual power. Steve Galagher, whose life is devoted to helping men overcome sexual addiction, writes:

> Being brutally honest with oneself is crucial, but it is only the beginning. One man who had been convicted for attempted rape, but later struggled his way out of sexual addiction said, "If you don't want to get rid of the problem, confess it only to God. If you want to get rid of the problem confess it to another person. And if you really want to get rid of the problem, keep yourself accountable." Yet another man who is now living in victory said, "I confessed my sin to God for years. I mean, I poured my heart out, begging for his forgiveness, but it was within weeks of starting to confess to another brother, that I obtained victory."[38]

May I suggest that the power of these groups is the result of following exactly what Paul wrote to the church at Ephesus about discipleship so long ago? *Speaking the truth in love we are to grow up into him who is the head, into Christ* (4:15-16).

God never intended believers to fight their spiritual battles alone. Indeed the very ferocity of some of those battles is what drives men to bring their struggle into the open and connect with some fellow strugglers. Nate Larkin, the founder of the Samson Society support groups says,

> I have come to realize that my sexual addiction was actually doing me a favor. It drove me to stop trying to live the Christian life on my own. I can't do it. I can't conquer my addiction on my own. Now I experience a richness in my life because of my connection with my brothers that I wouldn't trade for the world. Someday I will die. And I will be carried in death by them, the same way I was carried in life by them.[39]

What about you? Are the friends who will one day carry you in death, battle buddies who are carrying you right now in life?

Group Discussion Guide

1. Consider the church functioning as *organization*—in what ways are the preaching of the Word, administration of the sacraments, exercise of church discipline and shepherding of the flock central to the disciple-making process?
2. Consider the church functioning as *organism*—the body building itself up through *speaking the truth in love*. Have you noticed that when church members are not connected in the body, there is too much pressure on the leaders to meet nearly all of the members' relational needs through their shepherding?
3. In your setting, is your church functioning better as *organization* or as *organism?*
4. What parts of the "speaking the truth in love" explanation stood out the most to you?

Check #1: What encouragements or successes have you had this past week?

Check #2: What biblical insight or verse from your quiet time has stood out recently?

Check #3: What has been the most difficult part of being the spiritual leader at home lately?

Check #6: What spiritual battles can I help you fight through my prayer for you?

During the week: Prayerfully consider the depth of your own brotherhood connections. Are you talking honestly with a few brothers *about how you are applying scripture in your everyday life*? What steps could you take to deepen your connection with some brothers? What can your group do to help the other men in the church be better connected? Don't forget to pray for the spiritual battles of the men in your group.

Chapter 8

I've Got Your Back

During my time flying fighters for the Navy, our byline was "First in. Last out." The fighters escorted everybody else into the target area. We'd engage the enemy to keep them occupied, so the bombers could come in, drop their bombs, and get out. So, we'd keep the enemy fighting. Our dog fighting—shooting missiles and guns—would keep the enemy tied up so the bombers, who were not well armed, could get themselves out and back to the ship. First in. Last out.

Your biggest trouble, though, was if you got in that fur ball with the enemy and you lost your wingman. If you're out there solo you are dead meat. Because in the middle of all that, you've got to keep your eye on the enemy in front while realizing there's probably an enemy at what is called your six o'clock.

You've got one at your twelve o'clock. You've got one at your six and probably one's coming in at your three and your nine. And if you don't have another guy looking over your shoulder saying, "Be careful. You're vulnerable here. Be careful. Be careful," you're going to get shot.

I've spent too much time in my office, both in my squadron, and now in my church office, sitting across from a man who told me, "I got shot." And I say, "Where was your wingman?"

And he says, "Don't have any." A believer who is vulnerable out there, isolated, running by himself, is dead meat.[40]

*W*hy is it that so many Christian men are *vulnerable out there, isolated, running by themselves—dead meat*? This does not happen while men are still in the first life stage of discipleship—spiritual boot camp—where they usually have a speak-the-truth-in-love connection with other brothers. It is *after a young believer has completed a structured training program* and moved on to the spiritual adulthood stage of discipleship that **today's church is failing him**.

This is the life stage where a soldier spends most of his career and a believer spends most of his life. But usually, churches have no ongoing way to help men or women remain connected in the speak-the-truth-in-love relationships that are vital for continued spiritual growth. **This book is written to help churches fill this need!**

The Limitations of Men's Bible Study

The best vehicle for ongoing life-on-life discipleship is often a weekly men's Bible study. In fact you may be reading *Got Your Back* because your men's bible study is studying it together. This is an excellent way to help the men of your church begin to realize that God doesn't want them fighting their spiritual battles alone. It helps them begin, step by step, to be more vulnerable about their own spiritual battles and support other men in theirs. But as good as men's bible studies are for life-on-life discipleship, we need to be aware of their limitations. Here are several:

1. Even the best churches rarely have more than fifteen percent of their men regularly attending weekly men's studies, leaving a very high percentage of their men disconnected. Most men whose children are still at home don't want to spend one night of the week going to a men's Bible study. In some settings, a before-work study can be effective, since men would rather deprive themselves of a little sleep than be away from their homes in the evening. However, many times a man's long commute time or early morning work schedule makes a pre-work study impractical.

2. For those who can attend a men's Bible study, typically eighty-five percent of their time is spent discussing the content of what they are studying, with little thought given to how it impacts a man's walk with Christ. The questions in the study are not designed to help men *apply* what they learn to everyday discipleship, and little time is given in the meeting to *discussing spiritual battles*. Usually fifteen minutes are taken at the end for sharing rushed, superficial, prayer requests followed by a hurried time of prayer.

3. Many men's Bible studies are simply too large for much time to be spent focusing on each other's spiritual battles. Even if a group of six devoted a full twenty minutes to sharing prayer requests and then actually praying, each guy would have just three minutes and twenty seconds. Into this miniscule time segment, he would have to cram his request and the circumstances surrounding it, other's insightful and perhaps encouraging comments, his response to those comments, and time for the group members to pray together for his need.

An existing men's study can overcome these limitations to some degree by adjusting the study questions to focus on application, and by devoting more time to prayer for each other's spiritual battles. Groups larger than five can also be split into twos or threes for this prayer time. In fact many men's Bible study groups have studied this book, and begun using the *Check 6* questions in the appendix to generate life-related discussion, support, and a prayer time focused on helping each other with their spiritual battles.

Since men's small group bible studies are so limited, is there another structure that can help isolated men build the, speak-the-truth-in-love brotherhood connections they need? There is, and it is changing men's lives in the twenty-first century!

Filling the Gap: A New Structure

Someone has said, "The average man in today's Bible-believing church is educated way beyond his level of obedience." I agree. After the spiritual boot camp training phase of spiritual warfare, believers move into the *everyday combat* phase. Beyond the traditional men's Bible study, what meeting structure can enable a better time investment to help men with their spiritual battles?

The new structure that God is enabling many men to forge has been variously called, "Check 6 partners," "brothers in the battle," "battle buddies," "triads," "Jonathan and David relationships," and "accountability partners." It is a small group of guys gathered to share their spiritual battles, apply life-related Biblical principles, and fight for each other in prayer.

We've been helping such groups succeed, over the last nine years. Through trial and error, principles in the rest of this chapter have been refined by the fire of reality—the reality of time shortages and men's resistance to vulnerability, the fact that relationships can be fostered but not programmed, but also the reality of God's Spirit moving in men's hearts convicting them that they need a relationship like Jesus had with his closest friends, Peter, James, and John. *Unlike most discipleship programs, which correspond to the Army's boot camp, these life-on-life relationships correspond to a soldier's combat group, where he is assigned his everyday mission.*

Characteristics of a Spiritual Combat Group

The first distinguishing characteristic of a "combat-oriented" group is that at least eighty, if not one hundred percent of the time is devoted to discussion and prayer for *each other's spiritual battles*. Our *Check 6* groups are designed for men who are extremely busy just coping with life. They don't have the time for a deep, lengthy, Bible study, but these men know they need connection in the body for encouragement, replenishing, and accountability. After some initial small talk, the discussion is quickly focused onto their spiritual life by a guideline of the six questions, or other matters that surface related to their walk with God.

The second distinguishing characteristic of combat groups is that they are not built around older believers mentoring or teaching younger ones. They are based on the Eph. 4 call to *mutual discipleship*. Believe it or not, this characteristic is enormously freeing for believers over forty-five. The older men associate "discipling" with having a near one hundred percent success rate in their sanctification. Many of us are way too aware of our sin to presume to be a "discipler" of a younger man.

But these same men are responding in droves to the invitation to connect with a few guys for *mutual discipleship*. Not surprisingly, younger men in these connections learn greatly from the older guys. But the older guys learn much from the younger ones as well! The body is functioning as *organism*.

The collegial discipleship model is especially attractive to the under forty-five crowd. Numerous workplace studies comparing Baby Boomers to Millennials/Gen Y-ers reveal that Boomers are more hierarchical, whereas their adult children more egalitarian.

> A new poll reveals just how different Gen Y workers are from their Baby Boomer forefathers...They're more likely than average to think the boss could learn a thing or two from their young employees...Millennials see the work environment as flat. Vineet Nayer, the CEO of HCL Technologies says that Millennials "have little interest in hierarchy and are not particularly impressed by the titles and positions within the traditional pyramid structure." In the workplace, Millennials see no reason for a strict hierarchy.... An "ideocracy" should reign in the workplace, most Millennials believe, in which everyone should be heard from and the best ideas win out, regardless of who has been on the job longer, or who has a corner office.[41]

As a Baby Boomer, I wonder if the hierarchical nature of my age group has jaundiced our vision of the discipleship methodology in Scripture, causing us to assume the mentor/multiplication model is normative. In the twenty-first century environment, Millennials and Gen Y-ers believe they have something to offer in a discipleship arrangement, and the collegial discipleship approach of combat groups has been quite attractive to them.

The Origin and Success of *Check 6* Partnerships

An ideal structure for a "combat-focused" connection is what our ministry calls a *Check 6* partnership. Some years ago I met with a former

Marine helicopter pilot named Don Sampson who had become a church planter. He explained the reason for meeting:

> Gary, I have inherited two very strong home groups from the mother church of our church plant. But having been around men my whole adult life, I know that men simply don't open up about what is happening in their spiritual life in a mixed group. However, adding a men's Bible study another night of the week is not the answer. Most of my guys commute ninety minutes each way up to the Pentagon and back. They are already attending a weekly home group. They are not going to give up another night of the week for a men's Bible study.
>
> You know, since so many of my men work within one metro-stop of each other near the Pentagon, I wonder if it would work to get them together at lunch. But they would only have sixty minutes, not long enough to do a Bible study. Gary, could you write a series of questions they could use to be the agenda of their lunch meetings? And with only sixty minutes, we need to keep the groups size down. Let's aim for 2-4 men.

I returned to Don with six prayerfully designed questions to help his guys watch each other's back, which in the military is known as your *six*. We printed a pocket tri-fold called *Check 6*, which included the six basic questions along with a prayer card for each other's prayer requests. Don challenged his men to meet with a brother or two at lunch and start using the *Check 6* questions as the lunch agenda. From those lunches the men began to pray for each other's spiritual battles during the week.

Interest in the *Check 6* tri-fold spread quickly. As we made this tool available, we would receive feedback like these comments from Chris Braddy, Field Staff Representative for Officers' Christian Fellowship at Quantico.

> Every marine knows he needs a friend to watch his back. I have been using the *Check 6* tri-fold for my own personal accountability with a partner ever since I discovered it.

> *Check 6* is such a great tool to facilitate brotherhood
> and accountability that I hand out as many as I can to the
> men passing through Quantico. These things are all over
> the planet!
>   Marines recognize the value of structure to help them
> build good habits. *The Check 6* program provides that
> kind of structure for brothers in the spiritual battle.

After a church wanted to put copies of *Check 6* in their bulletin on Father's Day for every man in the church, (not a very effective strategy), I decided to write a sixty-page booklet, called *Forging Bonds of Brotherhood* (the pre-curser to this book), with the single purpose of persuading a Christian man that God never intended him to fight his spiritual battles alone. We praise God that since then, by word of mouth, over thirty-eight hundred copies of *Check 6* and *Forging Bonds of Brotherhood* have found their way into men's lives.

As I have had the privilege of challenging men from hundreds of churches to get connected to other men in s*peak-the- truth-in-love* relationships, numerous men, who have completed basic training discipleship programs, have decided to transition to relationships more for *spiritual combat* than study. Several men's ministry leaders who had taken their men through the three years of Men's Fraternity have found *Check 6* partnerships to be the ideal follow-up connection for their men. In the Men's Fraternity format, men listened to a thirty-minute video and then had twenty minutes of discussion around their table applying what they learned. This format fits the *speak-the-truth-in-love* requirement for true discipleship. But after three years, many men are ready to switch to a connection with men that has less time devoted to content presentation and more time devoted to sharing spiritual battles. They've begun *Check 6* groups.

Check 6 partnerships are formed when two to four men begin to gather weekly to share their lives and spiritual battles with each other. The *Check 6* questions are intended to be used in a sixty minute time block when there is not time for a full men's Bible study. (They can also be used as the *spiritual battle prayer request* component of a men's study.) *Check 6* partnerships may be formed by guys at breakfast on the way to work, over lunch during the workday, by giving the men regular time alone at a couples' study, through a weekly phone appointment, or by connecting at some other convenient time.

Perhaps the best way to bring the characteristic of such groups into clear focus is by way of contrast to the typical Bible study in today's church. A *Check 6* partnership is:

1. **Not a couples' group, but a band of brothers**. As one man said to me, "I'm not going to unzip my life very far in front of some other guy's wife. I find it hard enough to open up to my own wife! Plus my battle buds and I spent a lot of our time trying to help each other understand and better love our wives. Let me tell you something. Guys do not go very deep in mixed groups." As wonderful as the small group movement of the past sixty years has been, it has suffered from a serious flaw, in my view. It has failed to recognize that men cannot find the connection they need with other men in mixed groups.

2. **Not a two-hour Bible study, but a one-hour breakfast, lunch, or phone call.** Most men who are already in a couples' home group with their wives one night a week are not going to come home from work and turn around to go back out to a men's study another night of the week. *Often that's the only meeting structure available to men.* They have to either go to studies twice a week or choose between a couples' and men's study. For some men, meeting one of the men from his couples' study for breakfast on the way to work or at lunch provides the best of both worlds.

3. **Not an evening away from your family, but an hour from your work day.** In the twenty-first century, men and women who want to regularly workout would much rather do so during lunch or on the way home from work than get home and then turn around and go back out to the gym. In other words they would like to attach their workout to their work day. We are finding that around the nation, men feel the same way about the discipline of meeting weekly to focus on each other's spiritual battles. Fitting an hour-long *Check 6* breakfast or lunch into their workday makes connecting to some brothers doable, especially those who live near cities with heavy commuter traffic.

4. **Not 6-8 guys, but 2-4 guys.** Following the pattern of Jesus' relationship with Peter, James, and John or Jonathan's with David, *Check*

6 partners discover that if the group is larger than five, there simply is not enough time in sixty minutes for each guy to talk about how he is doing in his walk with Christ, respond to a few questions, and pray together. Larger groups can use the *Check 6* questions; they just don't have enough time to go very deep in sixty minutes.

5. **Not focused on learning, but focused on fighting**. Those in *Check 6* groups are extremely busy. Out of commitment to Christ and conviction that every believer needs to be connected in the body, they have responded to the challenge to give one hour a week to building a *speaking-the-truth-in-love* connection. They receive their academic book knowledge through hearing the sermon in Sunday worship, Christian radio, and other speaker downloads. What they want is life knowledge, which they get in their *Check 6* life-on-life connections by walking with other men.

6. **Not a meeting agenda that generates opinions, but a meeting agenda that generates connection as brothers.** Being friends with some Christian guys who share their opinions about a biblical text or a book is great, but it is a luxury for which *Check 6* partners don't usually have time. They want relationships that get down to the nuts and bolts of fighting their sinful nature, trying to love their family members well, and trying to keep their affections set on Christ instead of the idols of the world, which seek to steal them away. Of course it takes time to build such wingman connections—but that is where *Check 6* partners want to go. They want a brother fighting beside them who has their back. They want a brother to pick them up and encourage them when they fall, and they want to be that bother to some other men.

Over the past several years we have both succeeded and failed as we sought to help Christian men connect in combat-focused relationships like *Check 6* partnerships. This revision of the original booklet, *Forging Bonds of Brotherhood*, and the original *Check 6* questions reflect what we have learned in the process. Below is the revised *Check 6*. Feel free to download these questions at www.forgingbonds.org. (We no longer offer it as a tri-fold, because of the electronic nature of e-books).

Check 6 **Questions**

<u>Check #1</u>: **What encouragements or successes have you had this past week?**

Romans 12:15 commands, "Rejoice with those who rejoice." Celebrating each other's successes is an indispensable way to begin the time of sharing. Most Christian men feel beaten down by the world. Things don't always go as they would like at work, they generally feel like failures on the home front, and they usually feel like have had more defeats than victories in their spiritual lives. These men have stepped up and joined an accountability group—but they need a lot more than nagging.

Paul instructs us in I Thess. 5:11 to "Encourage each other and build each other up," and in Romans 12:10, "Be devoted to one another in brotherly love. Honor one another above yourselves." Just as Jonathan took off his royal robe and put it on David, *Check 6* brothers are committed to honoring one another. This is more than just a nice way to open the meeting; this is a heart-driven commitment!

A few months ago, I was on my way to breakfast with one of my battle buddies. Tom is a senior manager at Lockheed Martin and the most competent man I know. If I were jumping out of a plane I would want either Jesus or Tom to have checked out my parachute. Yet Tom struggles because his wife doesn't really realize how much he needs her respect. On the way to breakfast I thought, "Tom and I haven't asked that first question in a long time. I'm going to ask Tom, 'What encouragements or successes have you had in the past week?'"

He answered, "Funny that you would ask. I just had my performance review, and I received the highest possible rating that Lockheed Martin gives." Knowing Tom, he probably hadn't even mentioned this to anyone else. I'm so glad I asked that question to celebrate the way he had pleased Christ.

<u>Check #2</u>: **What Biblical insight or verse from your quiet time has stood out to you recently?**

This question builds a measure of accountability to be spending time in Christ's presence and Word regularly without becoming legalistic.

Jesus said, *"Abide in me and I will abide in you. No branch can bear fruit by itself; it must abide in the vine. Neither can you bear fruit unless you abide in me. I am the vine; you are the branches. If a man abides in me and I in him, he bear much fruit; apart from me you can do nothing"* (John 15:4). The Greek word, for "abide" means "stay connected." Jesus is saying that the foundation for the whole Christian life and prerequisite for true fruitfulness is maintaining our relationship with him. That is what having a daily quiet time is about.

Check 6 partnerships are intentionally structured with the three components Paul identifies in Eph 4:15: 1) speaking, 2) the truth, 3) in love. *Check 6* groups do not have time for a full study, **so this question is the way we get the application of Scripture into the forefront of conversation.**

This important step is also based upon Paul's admonition to the Christians at Colossae, "Let the word of Christ dwell in you richly as you teach and admonish one another with all wisdom and as you sing psalms, hymns and spiritual songs…" (Col. 3:16.). "You" is plural, indicating that Paul is not talking about an individual memorizing Scripture (as beneficial as that is), but about discussion among the believers that is centered in God's Word.

Proverbs 27:17 says, "As iron sharpens iron, so one man sharpens another." The tool which the Holy Spirit uses to sharpen us is the sword of the Spirit, i.e., the Word of God. So, this question is a way of putting God's Word into the hands of God's Spirit to build men up as they meet together. And, it is astonishing to see what he does.

Check #3: **What has been the most difficult part of being the spiritual leader at home lately?** (See Appendix #1 for tools to help with leading at home.)

Surveys indicate that married Christian men most want help in the area of their marriages. Leadership of any kind is a lonely position to hold, especially spiritual leadership of our homes. Jesus set the bar high for loving our wives—loving them as Jesus loves us. Most men struggle to understand the needs of their wives and to love their wives sacrificially, denying themselves. They don't know what it means to "lead" their wives and have only a vague idea of what they should be doing with their kids.

Few of us had role models; if we are doing anything it is usually flying by the seat of our pants. This question is designed to help men open up about their leadership challenges in their families and keep them focused on their loved ones' needs.

The following honest conversation explains why we need each other's help in this critical arena: "Gary, my wife told me the day after our wedding that she had made a mistake in marrying me. As Christians, we're committed to staying married. But the last few years have been a struggle."

"Bill, what specifically can I be praying for your marriage?"

"I know that I need to be less critical of my wife, but it is hard to find the strength when I know she thinks she made a mistake marrying me. *Things seemed to be going the best they have in a long while last fall when I was attending Tuesday night men's study.* I found more motivation to try harder and I was pushed to think about things I wouldn't have read on my own. Actually, our relationship was doing much better last fall." Most married *Check 6* partners spend a lot of time helping each other better love their wives.

Single men usually expect to be married one day and don't mind part of the discussion focused on marriage challenges. This question might provide them the opportunity to share a particular concern they have in a dating relationship or with their family of origin.

Check #4: **Personal Accountability: Choose what you want your brother(s) to ask you about.** (See Appendix #2 for a list of helpful accountability questions.)

In Ephesians 5:21, Paul commands us, "Submit to one another out of reverence for Christ." Paul establishes the general principle of accountability to one another before he addresses specific relationships such as husband/wife and slave/master. Paul further teaches us that part of our responsibility to others in the body is to *admonish* them as we speak the truth in love. Col. 3:16 says "Let the word of Christ dwell in you richly as you teach and *admonish one another* with all wisdom." James also implies accountability to one another when he says, "Therefore, confess your sins to each other, and pray for each other" (James 5:16).

Part of being a *Check 6* brother is acknowledging our own need for accountability and willingness to help our other brothers by holding them accountable as well. In the invisible, spiritual world, a brother I've asked to watch my back cannot usually *see* my sinful nature overpowering me; I must *tell him* about it. Actually having my brother's back means that he has requested that I regularly *ask* him how some spiritual battle is going.

The concept of accountability is often misunderstood, so we need to make some clarifications. The form of accountability practiced by *Check 6* brothers is *relational* accountability, which is different from *structural* accountability, the kind exercised by the church leadership. *Relational* accountability has two components: *trust* which is *earned*, and *an invitation* which is *given*.

When I become a *Check 6* brother, I am *asking* the other brothers to hold me accountable on a subject of *my* choosing. They are not *demanding the right*. None of us assumes that we have a right to hold our brother accountable. Rather, we have been asked by him to do so, and we have agreed. This distinction is important because it determines the right tone for the accountability questions. This tone is that of serving (even though it may mean asking tough questions), not one of demanding or condemning. Unless I have the responsibility as a church officer, under normal circumstances I earn the right to admonish a believer by being committed to him as a brother.

Check 6 accountability is NOT about making it your business to point your finger at others. Referring to accountability, Chuck Swindoll writes, "I'm talking about brothers who love you too much to let you play in dangerous traffic. They also love you too much to let you start believing in your own stuff. When they spot conceit rearing its head, they say so. But they also love you too much to let you be too hard on yourself."[42]

The original *Check 6* tri-fold had so many accountability questions that it was very difficult to get through them. We also discovered that early in a brotherhood connection, before a sufficient level of trust has been built, being asked each week, "Have you looked at sexually explicit material?" was scaring twenty-first century men away from participation. The new generation *Check 6* approach is to resolve both problems by challenging every *Check 6* member to choose *his own accountability question*. Choosing one himself allows each brother to be as personal as he is comfortable being and fits the time constraints of the meeting. We strongly recommend however that *Check 6* partners periodically review a carefully thought out list of accountability questions in Appendix #2.

<u>Check #5</u>: **What non-believers are you building relationships with and how can I pray for your strategy to share Christ with them?**

One of the most encouraging changes in the twenty-first century Evangelical church is the recovery of mercy ministry. Many churches are being intentional about seeking out the poor, the disenfranchised, the broken in their communities and sharing with them the mercy, generosity, and love of Christ. *Check 6* brothers need to challenge each other to be engaged in such mercy ministry and stand with them in it.

On the other hand, one of the most disturbing facts about modern Christians is that most of us have never led anyone to faith in Christ. We are much more comfortable being the keepers of the aquarium than fishers of men. Our self-centered, hard hearts are very different from Christ's, who wept over the lost.

In my life, my faithfulness in building relationships with the lost and seeking ways to share Christ with them stands or falls according to my prayer life. When I faithfully pray for opportunities to build relationships with lost neighbors, relatives, and friends, God provides them! When *Check 6* brothers begin to pray specifically for such opportunities, it is amazing to watch what God does.

A few years ago, I shared my concern with my *Check 6* brother that I was not sharing the gospel enough. We began to pray. Within a month or so, I was contacted by the pregnancy center our church had helped to start. They regularly provided a class for expectant mothers and wondered if I would do a class for the babies' fathers. This class provided a great opportunity to seek to winsomely share Christ with these young dads.

I had to give up leading the class after a few years. Before long, I again felt like I needed to share the gospel more. Phil and I began to pray, and within a few weeks, one of the dads I'd met through the pregnancy center class emailed me wanting help with his marriage. My wife and I started to meet with him and his wife. We talked about marriage but pointed them to Christ. I gave him a copy of *Mere Christianity*, and he either committed or re-committed his life to Christ (only God knows which it was).

In more recent months my *Check 6* partnership prayers for each other's outreach have led to many opportunities: a long conversation with a racquetball partner about Christianity and the biblical world and life view; an intentional effort to befriend a man living with the woman who is a next door neighbor; conversations at a sub shop with the owner; and a clear gospel presentation to a family friend, followed by ongoing conversations at a few Maryland basketball games.

There are many things about prayer that I don't know. But there is one thing I do know. When *Check 6* partners are intentional about asking God to provide opportunities to reach out, build relationships with non-believers, and share Christ—God answers those prayers! Christian men today need to be a lot more intentional about reaching those who don't know Christ.

Check #6: **What other spiritual battles can I help you fight through my prayer for you?**

Check 6 brothers refuse to be blind to spiritual reality. As we saw in the first chapter, we must wage a three-front war against our sinful nature, the world, and the devil. To follow King Jesus is to enlist in his cause—the establishment of his kingdom of righteousness over planet earth. That rule is to begin in my own heart with my loyalty to him—loving him with all of my heart and mind and soul and strength. That kingdom rule is to move outward to my heart attitudes, replacing pride with a recognition of my spiritual poverty, envy of the wicked with tears of grief for the way sin destroys, the need to be in control with surrender to Christ's control, etc. That kingdom rule then moves outward to my marriage and family relationships, my workplace, neighborhood, and culture. At every place in this world that Christ claims as his own there is a conflict between the Kingdom of Darkness and the Kingdom of Light.

In the context of discussing the Christian's fierce battle against the spiritual forces of evil in the heavenly realms, Paul commands us to be sure we have on the correct armor, and then to fight. How? In prayer. "And pray in the spirit on all occasions with all kinds of prayers and requests. With this in mind, be alert and always keep on praying for all the saints." In Mark 9:14-29, Jesus' disciples are not able to cast out a demon. When they ask Jesus why not, He said, "This kind cannot be driven out by anything but prayer." In Jesus' mind, prayer is the ultimate weapon in the battle with Satan. *Check 6* brothers are brothers-in-arms!! They fight for each other and each other's families on their knees.

In Exodus 17, Scripture gives a great picture of the power of prayer. As it so often does, the Old Testament gives us a physical picture of spiritual realities. Moses, with the staff of God in his hand, goes to the top of a hill overlooking a valley where Joshua and Israel's army meet the Amalekites in a pitched battle. When Moses raises his arms in prayer, holding the staff of God, Joshua and the Israelites prevail in the battle. But Moses' arms grow heavy. When he lowers them, the Amalekites begin to prevail. So, the men with Moses take a stone and put it under Moses for a seat, while Aaron and Hur hold up his hands, one on each side of him. With Moses' arms raised in prayer, Joshua and the Israelites prevail until sunset, overwhelming the Amalekites.

What a dramatic picture of the impact of prayer! Every man has loved ones down in the valley fighting spiritual battles against their sinful nature, the world that wants to squeeze them into its mold, and the devil. If we support them in prayer, those loved ones will win some battles that they will otherwise lose. But we, like Moses, get weary of the position of spiritual leadership and the need to keep battling in prayer. We need a few brothers to come under our arms and hold them up so we can continue on.

By their very nature, *Check 6* groups are designed to be about *combat*. They are life-on-life, *speak-the-truth-in-love* battle buddies who are trying to help each other win a few more spiritual battles, becoming a little bit more like Jesus and so honoring him. *Check 6* brothers put their love into action by praying for each other's spiritual struggles. In fact, depending on time constraints, many *Check 6* partners end their breakfast or lunch meeting by heading to the car for a time of intercessory prayer or praying at length right there in the restaurant or on the phone.

Scripture promises us, "Tremendous power is made available through a good man's earnest prayer" (James 5:16 J. B. Phillips). Be assured, our prayers for each other's spiritual battles matter!

The *Check 6* Covenant

In our examination of Jonathan's relationship with David, we saw the value of entering into a covenant with one another. Depending on how structured your *Check 6* connection is, you may want to ask the brothers to make a covenant with one another that includes these commitments.

A. *I commit to creating a climate of encouragement, safety and trust in the group.*
B. *I commit to keeping what is shared in the group confidential.*
C. *I commit to allowing every brother in the group the freedom not to answer a question he considers too personal.*
D. *I commit to be accountable to pray for each other during the week.*

In the race and pace of twenty-first century life, a new approach to helping men connect as brothers has immerged. Instead of repeating a three-year, content-heavy program of basic discipleship or basic masculinity, men are finding their way into groups where over seventy-five percent of the meeting time is focused on their walk with Christ. Small groups of two to four men are meeting for sixty minutes, often attached to their workday, finding out how they can support each other in their daily spiritual battles.

These are brothers who, like Jonathan and David, are intentional about their commitment to each other. It is a commitment defined by an unshakable loyalty to each other that revels in honoring one another, speaking the truth to one another, fighting spiritual battles for one another, and watching one another's six. It is a band of brothers with whom, like Jesus, we share what is happening in our closest relationships, reveal more and more of our real selves, and expect help in our difficult times.

Think for a moment about what would happen in your church if every man had a *Check 6* connection to a few brothers who were helping him fight his spiritual battles and watching his back. What would happen in your city if every Christian man had such a connection?

The next chapter tells the story of how RIGHT NOW individual men are forging this kind of bond of brotherhood across the land and how church leaders are helping their men do it.

Group Discussion Guide

1. In your own words, what are the distinguishing characteristics of a connection with some brothers that is more of a "combat group" than a typical men's Bible study or discipleship training?
2. Looking back at the description of a *Check 6* connection, what aspects of it do you think explain why it has been so successful?
3. If you are using this book for a men's study, do you have any ideas about how your group might focus a little more on your spiritual battles?

<u>Check #1</u>: What encouragements or successes have you had this past week?

<u>Check #2</u>: What Biblical insight or verse from your quiet time has stood out recently?

<u>Check #3</u>: What has been the most difficult part of being the spiritual leader at home lately?

<u>Check #5</u>: What non-believers are you building relationships with and how can I pray for your strategy to share Christ with them?

<u>Check #6</u>: What spiritual battles can I help you fight through my prayer for you?

Chapter 9

Starting A *Check 6* Partnership

We need MEN to whom we can bare our souls. But it isn't going to happen with a group of guys you don't trust, who really aren't willing to go to battle with you. It's a long standing truth that there is never a more devoted group of men than those who have fought alongside one another, the men of your squadron, the guys in your foxhole. It will never be a large group, but we don't need a large group. We need a band of brothers willing to 'shed their blood' with us.[43]

*B*y now, I hope you agree with the above quote—we need men to whom we can bare our souls. The question is, how do I go from not having such close brothers to having them? Over the past eight years, here is *what has worked* to help men forge brotherhood connections.

Underlying Principles

1. It requires intentionality. Having such a brotherhood bond doesn't happen automatically in our fallen world. When Adam and Eve disobeyed God and sin came into the world, they sewed fig leaves together to hide their nakedness. Because sin has invaded our world, nakedness makes us uncomfortable, especially nakedness of soul, for two reasons. First, we are *ashamed*—we don't want others to see our sinful selves as we really are. Second, nakedness makes us *vulnerable*—we don't want to expose ourselves to the harm that can be inflicted upon us by other sinful humans. In a fallen world, we need clothing—walls surrounding and protecting our nakedness. Thus, we read in Genesis 3:21 that God clothed Adam and Eve.

However, the very walls we need to protect us in a fallen world also isolate us. That is why the status quo among Christian men is to have only superficial relationships. The wall of self-protection is there. So, Christian men will remain isolated unless *they take action* to build a small window through the wall into another man's life. They must be intentional about building such a friendship. Rarely will it fall out of the sky into their laps!

2. It requires time and determination to build trust. We gradually chisel away at the wall of self-protection by building trust. Bit by bit, as trust grows, our resistance to exposing our inner selves crumbles. The wall of protection is replaced by a window of trust. The *trust-building* process works over *time* like this:

> Jim reveals something about himself to Clint.
> Clint understands it, values it, and still respects Jim
> Clint then reveals something about himself.
> Jim must understand it, value it, and still respect Clint.
> Jim reveals something deeper about himself.
> Clint must understand it, value it, and still respect Jim.
> Clint reveals something deeper about himself.
> Jim must understand it, value it, and still respect Clint, etc.

Meanwhile, the other components required for *trust* to grow must be in place. These include caring about each other, maintaining confidentiality, being honest, treating each other with kindness, responding appropriately to what is shared, etc. If a brother bares his soul about his dying mother and during the next week, no one remembers to ask him about his mom, the trust level in the group will tank. The expectations we have of the group members increase because we want others in the group to be responsible for the information that has been revealed. If what we share is understood, is valued, and doesn't result in being disrespected, the trust level in the group will continue to grow.

93

The energy that keeps the process of forging bonds of brotherhood going forward is *determination*. You must be persuaded that Christian isolation is an oxymoron—that the call to be Christ's disciple is a call to connection with a band of brothers who know what is going on in your soul. That is the reason I wrote this book. **You** must be persuaded that unless you proactively forge a bond of brotherhood with some other men, you will be alone in your struggles, without the brother you need for encouragement, focus, strength, and accountability.

Without an unrelenting commitment to going the full distance in forging a bond of brotherhood, you will cut this process short. As the trust level grows, you will move from acquaintance to close friendship with a few guys and find it very, very comfortable to stop there. Your sinful, masculine heart resists vulnerability and accountability.

Without the resolve to keep chipping away at that wall until there is enough trust to share what is happening in your soul, you won't reach the level of brotherhood. You'll have some Christian buddies you like— but NOT *brothers-in-arms*. You'll find enjoyment from discussing above-the-waterline issues like work, politics, or sports, but NOT find the strength that comes from relating at the level of the soul. You'll have guys sitting beside you in a study or at a restaurant, but NOT fellow warriors fighting beside you in each other's battles. You will have failed to build the *speak-the-truth-in-love* connection that grows Christ's disciples up into him, the Head.

You will have settled for a cheap imitation; it is the mutual commitment to battle together for each other that binds the hearts of fellow-soldiers together. In their book about the Vietnam war, Hal Moore and Joe Galloway write,

> We discovered in that depressing, hellish place, where death was our constant companion, that we loved each other. We killed for each other, we died for each other, and we wept for each other. And in time we came to love each other as brothers. In battle our world shrank to the man on the left and the man on our right and the enemy all around....We learned to share our fears, our hopes, our dreams as readily as we shared what little else good came our way.[44]

What is true of physical warfare is true of the spiritual battle in which we are called to enlist. The riches that accompany the deepest level of masculine friendship belong only to those brothers whose faces are marred by the dust and sweat and blood of spiritual battle, who may come up short again and again, but who are in the fight...together.

3. It requires balancing the structured and organic dimensions of the relationships. On the one hand a *Check 6* partnership has some structure. It doesn't arise naturally but as a result of intentionality. The actual meetings themselves are structured by using the *Check 6* questions as a guideline and by a covenant of commitments to one another.

Yet in another sense, these partnerships are organic, real friendships. The *Check 6* questions are just training wheels to help men talk about their spiritual struggles consistently enough to become best friends. The six-question agenda should always be thrown out if some other issue needs to be in the forefront (which is quite often the case). A *Check 6* meeting should never be an over-programmed, cold, mechanical, response to six questions. In fact, in my *Check 6* relationships we rarely even refer to the questions. We are just best friends trying to love each other well, as brothers in Christ.

Ted Kluck and Dallas Jahncke tell the story of the growth of their friendship in their book, *Dallas and The Spitfire*.[45] Ted is a thirty-four year old father of two who'd been going to church his whole life. Dallas is a twenty-one-year-old former cocaine addict with a prison record. When they agreed to meet regularly for "discipleship" they realized that chatting once a week in a coffee shop was not their style. They decided instead to build their friendship around doing things together— at first sparring in Ted's basement boxing ring and then restoring an old Triumph Spitfire convertible. Over time, as their friendship grew, they began *speaking the truth in love*—that is talking with one another honestly about how they are applying and failing to apply Christ's teaching in their lives.

Men tend to build friendships shoulder to shoulder. My *Check 6* brothers are men to whom I originally grew close on the normal path of friendship. Phil, who grew up as a pastor's kid, was always very supportive of me and my family when I was his pastor. He and I got close

95

one spring when he volunteered to help me build a deck. He is also on the board of my ministry and his son married my daughter.

My other *Check 6* brother, Tom, has been equally devoted to serving me as his pastor in numerous practical ways. We grew close because of his personal commitment to do all of the repair work on my cars. He'd be under my car fixing something, I would be handing him a wrench, and we'd both be talking about our marriages and realizing how impossible it is to figure a woman out. These days Tom is too busy to take care of my cars, but he takes me to Maryland basketball games and meets me for breakfast. We've also tried to see if his pair of jet skis will go faster than sixty-five. (They do.)

These *speak-the-truth-in-love* connections, which Paul said build us up into Christ the Head, are real friendships, not mechanical, superficial, or programmed discussions. There needs to be this balance—part organic friendship that you *let happen* naturally, and part structured connection that you *make happen* by intentionality.

Even though a *Check 6* partnership is a real, organic, friendship, I have also seen the value of returning to the "structure" side of things from time-to-time lest we spend most of our time talking sports and politics. It is worth remembering to ask what has gone well this past week in each other's life, and what we are learning in Scripture. It is valuable to remind each other of what we are holding each other accountable, and to be intentional about praying for each other's outreach opportunities. At times we also need to confess our sins to one another.

Practical Steps for Forging A *Check 6* Partnership

Step 1: **Take an honest inventory of your life.** Do you have a brother who is helping you fight your spiritual battles? Do you have a brother who even knows what your spiritual battles are? If you are in a men's Bible study, do you have a structure that takes you deep enough into each other's lives that you share at the soul level. Do you have a few things you are holding each other accountable for? Are you aware of the cost to yourself, your family, and the Lord's reputation if you remain isolated?

Step 2: **Be brutally honest about why you have no brotherhood relationships.** If you are not meeting regularly with a brother or band of brothers for encouragement and strength, don't blame your busy schedule and lack of time. You have all the time there is! The issue is what you make a priority. Don't blame the demands of work. Three years after you quit your job, few of your coworkers will even remember your name. Don't blame your wife who doesn't want you away from her for one more meeting. No one is suggesting that you should steal an hour a week from time with her in order to have male connection. It's not that you *can't* form a band of brothers, it's that you *haven't wanted to* badly enough to do it.

You also may not have true brotherhood relationships even if you are meeting with some other men, because you are not getting to the level of soul issues. In this case, the *Check 6* questions may be just the help you need.

<u>Step 3</u>: **Decide that you are willing to pay the price for God's best.** Forging a bond of brotherhood, though profoundly satisfying to the masculine soul, is not easy. Potential schedule conflicts will arise constantly. Other responsibilities will compete with this priority. More sinister will be your sinful nature's resistance. You may think, "I don't need this group. I'm doing fine." On weeks when you've messed up, many excuses will cross your mind for skipping the meeting. We don't like accountability. We want to avoid the shame of admitting our sins.

But the alternative is to remain undisciplined and lazy, to stay with the status quo, and to be alone in your struggles. It is to choose "mediocrity" as the defining word for your commitment to Christ, concern for the lost, care for your family, and devotion to your wife.

<u>Step 4</u>: **Trust God to provide the brotherhood connection you need.** You may look at your schedule and conclude that it is totally impossible to find an hour per week to forge a brotherhood connection. That's okay. Ask the God of the impossible to provide a way, then think outside the box, keep praying, and wait to see what God does. He is more committed to you being connected in the body than you are!

One man heard this challenge and thought, "There is no way I could meet some guys for breakfast before work or for lunch at work. I am a full-time care giver, and my wife has Alzheimer's." But he continued to think about it.

Several months later, I was back visiting his church. He came bounding up to me and said, "You know what, Gary? I am talking almost every day to a man who has become my best friend!"

I asked, "What happened?"

He answered, "After your challenge, I started thinking about an old friend. We used to be in a Bible study together. I called him up, explained that I enjoyed our friendship, that I am tied to the house because of my wife's illness, and wondered if we could call each other on the phone once a week to share prayer requests. He thought that was a great idea. But you know what? We actually talk to each other by phone almost every day. Thanks so much for helping me discover the brotherhood connection I didn't know I needed."

Several pastors have told me that since most everyone now has free long distance, they have forged a brotherhood connection through a weekly phone call to an old seminary buddy. Such connections are ideal.

You may look at your schedule and say, "There is absolutely no way I have time to do this." Trust God to miraculously provide the time anyway. Many of us have been challenged in the midst of a church building program to make a "faith commitment" to trust that God will enable us to give a certain monthly amount to the building fund. We were challenged to "trust God" even though it seemed impossible to squeeze that extra amount from our budget. But somehow God worked it out!

Trust God in the same way to provide an extra hour/week and practical way to squeeze a brotherhood connection into your life. The benefits to you and your loved ones will be immeasurable.

<u>Step 5</u>: **Prayerfully choose the type of connection that fits you best.** Based upon your schedule and existing friendships, would a one-on-one, Jonathan and David relationship work best or forming a small band of brothers? If you are in an existing men's group, should the goal be to get the whole group to go deeper, or to piggy back off the group and go deeper with a few? If you are in a couples' group, what would work the best for you: setting aside some of that meeting time for some male prayer time or meeting regularly with one of those brothers outside the meeting? Ask God for one brother who will see the need for a deeper relationship with a few other Christian men.

Keep in mind that *Check 6* partnerships can't work if the logistics of getting together are too difficult. Over the long haul, weekly meetings are far superior to bi-weekly meetings, and monthly *Check 6* connections probably won't work at all. There is simply too much water that goes under the bridge in a month. Someone whose schedule and location match yours will usually work better than a closer friend whose schedule makes it hard to meet.

If you are married, talk this all over with your wife. She will have insight about both your schedule and the men with whom you might connect. Share with her some of the principles of this book or let her read it. Especially talk with her if you want some male time at the couples' study. If she is a real advocate of this idea, she can help persuade the other wives that men need time together, that *"Check 6"* (speak-the-truth-in-love) connections mean that their husbands are being challenged to better meet needs at home, and that time for same gender connection at the couples study means they are NOT away from their wives another night of the week.

One pair of brothers found that the freest time in their week was Sunday morning. After all, a man's body clock is usually programmed by his work week-schedule to awaken him early enough that he has a spare hour or two Sunday morning. Since getting the kids ready for church was not too heavy a burden for their wives, they found the best plan was to meet at the church twenty to thirty minutes before everyone else so they could pray together.

Step 6: **Decide what man or men with whom you want to try to connect and schedule a get-together:** If you want to meet with one man, invite him to breakfast or lunch. Usually this proceeds from a good discussion about walking with Christ. So, it is easy to say, *"It's been great talking—wish we had a little more time. Would grabbing you for breakfast or lunch sometime work?"* He may say, "No. Meeting around my work schedule won't work. But you know our kids seem to like playing with each other. Maybe our families could get together." There is no ONE SIZE FITS ALL way to help men forge brotherhood bonds.

If you want to invite a few guys to meet together, contact each one and say something like, *"Nate, I've been challenged with the idea that God doesn't want any man fighting his spiritual battles alone but how every man needs a brother or two to be praying for each other's battles. A few of us guys thought we'd try meeting once a week to give this a shot."*

Most likely your motivation for forming such a group and understanding of the way it might operate have been impacted by this book. The other men you are pursuing for connection need to have the same vision as yours, so you might want to to lend them your copy to browse through. The reason I wrote this short book is for this very purpose—to give a man a concrete vision—a picture of a favorable future that God wants him to have.

If the man or men are favorable, set a date for the first meeting.

<u>Step 7</u>: **At your first meeting:** <u>If you want to meet with *one man*,</u> *when you get together, be vulnerable about some of your* struggles. Ask how you might pray for him and ask for his prayer support for one of your battles. If it felt good getting together, you might say, "It's been good talking. Would you be interested in getting together again in a couple of weeks?" Often, it is best to start off meeting once a month or every other week. As the relationship grows, you might want to introduce him to this book—and the challenge to have a spiritual battle-buddy or two. As you grow closer, you may realize the need to attempt to meet weekly. (Because life has a way of interrupting our plans and the attempt to meet every week usually ends up at most three out of four). If that doesn't work, meeting every other week is better than no connection at all.

<u>If you want to invite a few guys to get together</u>, you will probably want to review and discuss the *Check 6* Covenant. Look over the *Check 6* questions. Review the ideas about leadership at home in Appendix 2, and the potential accountability questions in Appendix 3. Emphasize the fact that we choose those things for which we want our brothers to hold us accountable. A good starting place for accountability might be trying to read the Bible 5 days out of 7, or to pray more regularly for my wife and kids. Be sure to end the meeting on time. Share one spiritual battle you'd like the other brothers to pray about and set the time for the next meeting. You are launched!

Another quite common way to start the group is to read *Got Your Back* together, one chapter per week. As you know by now, this is written with discussion questions at the end of each chapter and starts adding one, new, Check 6 question each week, starting week 3.

Step 8: **Reinforce the relationships outside of the *Check 6* group.** Men tend to build relationships by doing things together, so look for opportunities! Your group might want to all help a brother with some house project one Saturday morning, go to a ball game together, travel to men's ministry events together, or do something socially together with your wives.

Prov. 17:17 tells us, "*A friend loves at all times and a brother is born for adversity.*" Use the phone or email during the week to make contact with a brother who is going through a tough time. Surround him with love and support. That is what forging a bond of brotherhood is about!

Step 9: **Persevere.** If the connection gets stale, you may want to change your agenda by discussing an article, a quote, or a chapter from a Christian book.

Continue to be intentional about going beneath the superficial to the place of our spiritual battles, or your *Check 6* group will become more like a group of golfing buddies than a band of fellow warriors who stand beside each other in their spiritual battles. Men need more than golfing buddies. Remember, if getting together with men for support and accountability were easy, you would already be doing it!

Group Discussion Guide

1. Why do you think it takes *intentionality* to forge a *Check 6* kind of friendship with a few men?
2. Why does it take time and determination to build trust with some potential *Check 6* partners?
3. In what ways do you think a *speak-the-truth-in-love* relationship (*Check 6* partnership) must balance structure and the non-structural, natural friendship elements?
4. If you are using this book for a men's study, what ideas do you have about how your group might continue to focus on your spiritual battles after you finish this book?

Check #1: What encouragements or successes have you had this past week?

Check #2: What Biblical insight or verse from your quiet time has stood out recently?

Check #3: What has been the most difficult part of being the spiritual leader lately?

Check # 5: What non-believers are you building relationships with and how can I pray for your strategy to share Christ with them?

Check #6: What spiritual battles can I help you fight through my prayer for you?

Chapter 10

Helping Your Men
Become a Band of Brothers

The poster represented one of the oldest and most famous orphanages in this country. Father Flanagan had captured the heart of the orphanage and the hearts of America in that well-known poster. In the background are the wide-open, storm-wracked skies of the American Midwest. An ominous storm brews in the direction from which two young urchins have just come. The younger boy clings to the back of the older boy. The two have evidently just knocked on the door of a farm house seeking shelter. A rather matronly figure has answered the door and apparently quizzed the boys a bit and made a comment about the fact that one is carrying the other.

The poster's caption is the words of the older boy's response. He says simply, *"He ain't heavy. He's my brother."*[46]

Over the years we have assisted hundreds of churches to help their men forge brotherhood bonds with one another. In this chapter, we want to observe the most common mistakes we have seen churches make in this process and then examine six practical steps your leadership team can take to help your men connect. You may not be an official leader of your church or men's ministry, but this chapter will help you help the isolated men of your church build the friendships they need.

How to Fail

Looking back over the past eight years, we've discovered one common formula for failing with this material: viewing this book and *Check 6* partnerships as a *program* for getting men connected. After reading the first six chapters of this book, many church leaders are highly motivated to help their men forge the bonds of brotherhood they need for discipleship. That is precisely the hope we have in writing them! However, the problem comes in thinking that such relationships can be manufactured. We've observed three pitfalls of the manufacturing/program mentality when it comes to using this material.

First, we've seen churches try to program the whole congregation, artificially dividing them into *Check 6* type partnerships from the top down. One church attempted to take one Sunday evening per month to gather its men together. They first met as a large group to hear the pastor provide some excellent biblical teaching about masculinity. Next, they were divided into small groups by ruling elders since each of the families in the church had been assigned a ruling elder. Then, after a discussion led by the elder, the men were further assigned a "foxhole buddy" with whom they were to share prayer requests.

Can you see why this didn't work? It failed because it imposed an artificial relational division from the top down. Instead of the option to choose an elder and discussion group, a man was assigned to the group led by his elder. His assigned foxhole buddy was someone who happened to be in the same elder's group.

I was a part of this effort and did not realize myself that it would fail. The intention was good. *Check 6* partnerships do have a programmatic component; there is intentionality and an agenda. This approach also tried to strengthen the elder's ties with the sheep under his care and recognized the value of men going deeper with just a few battle buddies.

Nevertheless, the approach did not succeed because it was too structured. It required all the elders to participate when some of their hearts were not in it. Most importantly, we realize looking back that a successful *Check 6* partnership must be a real, organic friendship among men who want to be together—genuine friends! Their connection can be **assisted**, but can't be **programmed** by the church.

The second way that a program mentality will cause *Check 6* partnerships to fail is that *programs* are expected to work quickly, at least within a few years. We have worked with several churches that experienced a flash-in-the-pan success helping their men in the church build *Check 6* connections. But for one reason or another, some churches didn't stick with the effort to keep challenging men to be connected.

One church had over twenty-five groups of two or three men meeting weekly for lunch using *Check 6*. Looking back now the pastor writes,

> We encouraged men to form accountability groups of two or three. The effort was launched with great fanfare at a special dinner for men. Almost every man who attended signed up to join an accountability group. The groups were very effective for those who participated, but it was not well organized or managed. Most of the groups eventually disbanded due to the inevitable turnover of people in our church and lack of oversight. [47]

Perhaps this experience should be considered a failed program. Or should it? In the pastor's words, *the groups were very effective for those who participated*.

The third way we have seen churches fail is because of unrealistic expectations about getting their men connected. Pastors and other men's leaders have become thoroughly persuaded (through this material!) that countless men in our churches are stunted in their spiritual growth into Christ the Head because they are not connected in the body. I agree, and more importantly I believe Jesus and Paul would. *But seeing a deep-rooted problem clearly is only the first step to solving it.* Countless Christian men will die without ever having a brother who knows what their true spiritual battles are.

Knowing the problem does not mean it is easy to solve it. A doctor may know his patient has cancer, but that doesn't mean the doctor can always cure it. The epidemic of male isolation is bringing destruction into many Christian men's lives today. But the reasons for male isolation are often deeply rooted and difficult to overcome.

We need to recognize that if we can help get a man to take one step closer to connection, God has used our effort. An empty-nester who is a little more vulnerable at a men's breakfast, acknowledging his son's marital problems may be the best we can do. An unconnected man who starts making more of an effort to come to men's events is a victory. A Stepping Up or Men's Fraternity group of men who strive to be a bit more vulnerable in their post-lecture discussion is a win. An adult Sunday school teacher who starts including more discussion, because he realizes the importance of connecting over the Word of God is progress. If exposing men to this material helps them take just the next step towards a wingman connection—we have succeeded.

This book is intended not so much to be a short term relational fix as a long term effort to change the DNA of the church one strand at time. It is an effort to steer an ocean liner, called the Church—to persuade church members and leaders that God never designed men to fight their spiritual battles alone.

Actually, viewed through this lens, the *Check 6* program mentioned above that at one point had twenty-five triads did not entirely fail. In a recent poll of his men, my pastor friend found that the one thing the men most wanted the church to provide to assist them in their discipleship was *accountability relationships*. Could it be that we changed the DNA of the church?

If church leaders are not going to succeed at building a "*Check 6* Accountability *Program*," how can they use these materials to help their men get better connected for encouragement and accountability? How do they change the DNA of the church so its corporate culture creates the expectation that the men of the church don't fight their spiritual battles alone, but have a battle buddy who has their back? Here is what we've learned.

How to See Results With This Material

1. **As leaders, model a commitment to having a *Check 6* kind of connection.** The more you and the rest of the leadership team at your church put into effect the principles of this book, the greater your impact will be with the rest of the men. Men learn best by watching other men. This principle has both a negative and a positive component.

On the negative side, if I were to identify one reason why nineteen out of twenty Christian men have no brother watching their back, it is because nineteen out of twenty *pastors* have no brother watching *their* back. Leaders reproduce themselves.

In all fairness, it must be said that pastors have the most to lose by confessing their secret sins. If word got out to his congregation that a pastor was unable to conquer his struggle with pornography, his ministry would probably be destroyed. Pastors today have good reason to be guarded about their personal struggles with sin. In fact I recommend that a pastor NOT be TOTALLY TRANSPARENT with his congregation. He should have a brother in his life with whom he can be transparent; but it must be a brother who is safe.

Modeling commitment to a *Check 6* brother in your personal life does NOT mean that pastors turn their church staff or elder board into mutual accountability partners, nor that men's ministry leaders become *Check 6* brothers to each other. *Check 6* partnerships cannot be imposed organizationally from the top down. Rather, what must be modeled is that the leader believes he needs a *speak-the-truth-in-love* brother, so he has one with whom he regularly connects. The model is *having* such a brother, not that the brother has *come from the leadership team* or even the same church.

Although responsibility for the current epidemic of male isolation needs to be squarely placed at the feet of today's pastors who are not modeling such connections, the exciting reality is that this pattern is changing. More and more pastors are connecting with an old friend from college, an army pal, or seminary buddy, reviving the old friendship, and using the availability of free long distance to talk regularly together.

But, what if your pastor and elders don't model this kind of connection? Remember that most don't. You can still have a major positive impact on the men in your church. If you are on the men's ministry leadership team, the starting point for impacting the rest of the men in your congregation is to get your leadership team to read through this book together and begin to implement these principles *in your own lives*. This is usually the most ideal way to impact the men of your church with the *Check 6* material.

This is the strategy followed by an assistant pastor named Trent at a church in Naples, FL. He discovered *Forging Bonds of Brotherhood* (original version of *Got Your Back*) as he was considering materials for a discipleship training program he designed for the young guys in his church. He bought ten copies, had the men in his discipleship class read them, then flew me down to Naples for a supper and class with his guys. Trent wanted me to build on the enthusiasm the guys had for the material and answer practical questions they had about building *Check 6* partnerships. This meeting helped cement their commitment to implementing what they learned. We talked about how to impact the overall men in the church and six months later, they ordered eighty copies of *Forging Bonds of Brotherhood*. Trent had the wisdom to let his core guys build brotherhood connections before casting the vision to the overall men of the church. This has been a common and effective pattern.

Another church, this one in central Virginia, used the *Forging Bonds of Brotherhood* material in their diaconal training. One of the deacons told me later, "Gary, this book is fantastic. It has practically started a revival among our deacons."

2. **Be sure your men's ministry is built on the foundation of grace**. In order to establish a safe climate for men to be vulnerable about their spiritual battles, the "corporate identity" of the men's ministry must be that we are the screw-ups of the church, but God loves us anyway. Steve Brown writes,

> The church is actually a place for people who are needy, afraid, confused, and quite sinful. But even more important than that, the church is a place for people who have been loved…and have no idea why. Each congregation is, as it were, a local chapter of "Sinners Anonymous."[48]

The men's ministry must view itself *not* as the guys who have it together but as the chief sinners and therefore the chief repenters in the church. Peter Scazzero, in his book, *The Emotionally Healthy Church* points to the parable of the prodigal son, reminding us:

> The younger son's brokenness is the picture of the Christian life. I must live there intentionally. Otherwise, I will end up being the older brother standing erect to the

right… He is kneeling because he cannot do life on his own. He is seriously dependent. He is very, very needy. We all are. We often forget that truth when things are going our way.[49]

3. **Continually cast a vision of brotherhood connection.** It is difficult to over-emphasize this step. The goal is to get every man in the church to buy-in to this idea: *God never intended a Christian man to fight his spiritual battles alone.* Until a man is persuaded of this truth, he will not have the inner drive he needs to forge a brotherhood bond. Even if a man's church has a program using *Check 6*, he has to commit to this idea himself or after the program, he'll return to isolation.

The power of ownership or getting others to "buy in" to a goal was explained to me by a friend who was one of the vice presidents of General Electric. He said, "Gary, on a 10 point scale, you could have an idea that is an 8. But, if you only get a 'buy in' of 3 by your leadership team, your value, when it comes to implementation, will only be 24. On the other hand, you could have an idea that is only a 5, but if you get a 'buy-in' of 8 in your organization, your value is 40.

Casting a vision of connection among brothers is the way to get a "buy-in" to the idea of forging a *Check 6* partnership. Casting a vision means simply to paint a picture of a better, possible future. When a man reads *Got Your Back*, our hope is for a man to say, "I want a brotherhood connection like that." When he hears about his pastor having an accountability partner, we want him so say, "I guess I need that too." When he hears a couple of men talk about how they forged a deep friendship using the *Check 6* questions, we want men to say, "I could do that." We've painted a picture of a future he could have. Below are seven ways men's leaders have been casting a vision of brotherhood connection.

A. Have men tell their stories. Wherever you spot a few men in *speak-the-truth-in-love* kinds of relationships, urge them to tell their stories. They might tell it at a men's breakfast or even in a worship service. It doesn't have to be guys using the *Check 6* questions. If they have forged a genuine bond of brotherhood and are willing to talk a little about it— their stories can cause a man to say, "I could do that, or "I need a brother like that."

I was invited to speak to about ninety guys at a Beast Feast at a church in Woodbridge VA on the topic, "Becoming a Band of Brothers." I thought my talk went well. But the real impact came not from my talk, but when two young guys stood up. One said, "Three years ago, when Gary was here, I picked up a copy of *Forging Bonds* and read through it. I gave a copy to my friend Bill. We knew we both like cycling, so now we ride together a lot and talk about how we're doing with Christ and stuff."

B. Give *Got Your Back* to the new men when they join the church. One men's ministry leader in Sacramento, CA got permission to visit each new members' class. He would drop in and say, "We really believe God doesn't want any man having to fight his battles alone. Here's a gift from the men's ministry that explains that. We know it takes time to get to know other guys. I just wanted to personally invite you to the men's breakfast next month." A great time to cast a vision for brotherhood connection is when a man is about to join the church.

C. Persuade the existing men's Bible studies to study *Got Your Back*. This is by far the most frequent way we have seen men buy into the principle that they need to be connected to a brother for encouragement and accountability. Several years ago, we added discussion questions to the original, sixty-page, *Forging Bonds of Brotherhood* book, turning it into a nine-week study. Since then, the most common number of copies ordered at one time from our website has been five or six—to be used in group studies. Many groups that complete the study start to use some of the *Check 6* questions as a regular part of their study. Sometimes, men who can no longer attend the study decide to start *Check 6* partnerships with a few guys. There is no "one size fits all," when it comes to building *speak-the-truth-in-love* relationships, but a great starting place is inviting existing men's studies to consider studying this book.

D. Use *Got Your Back* for one-on-one discipleship. The *Check 6* questions were originally designed for men to use to disciple one another over lunch. Since the only "discipleship structure" that most men were familiar with was full Bible study, I wrote *Forging Bonds of Brotherhood* so that a man who wanted to try a lunch hour commitment with another brother could "paint a picture" of how this would work. *Got Your Back,* the updated version of *Forging Bonds* remains a tool to show what meeting for a sixty minute breakfast, lunch, or phone call for mutual discipleship might look like. So, getting a friend to read it is a way to help him buy into the idea that he needs a *speak-the-truth-in-love* connection.

E. Set and communicate high expectations for the men of your church. Tom Joyce, the men's ministry pastor of Immanuel Church in Springfield, VA. has developed four *core competencies* that he wants to help every man at Immanuel achieve. These are:

1. For every man to be able to tell his personal story of how Jesus intersected his life.
2. For every man to understand and fulfill his biblical role as a man.
3. For every man to be committed to personal Bible study and prayer.
4. For every man to meet with another man for prayer, encouragement, and accountability.

Men love challenges. These, core, measurable competencies provide four targets on the wall for men to strive, in Christ, to reach.

F. Invite me to lead a weekend retreat, *Becoming a Band of Brothers*. I've been invited to lead many men's retreats and conferences, sharing the material in this book. Often the best way to challenge men with their need for a brotherhood connection is to get them on a weekend when this material is presented. Men often glean more in a weekend retreat than they will from reading a book, simply because they will never get around to reading the book. Also, a men's retreat on this topic gives them a taste of the very thing we are advertising!

Here are some of the things said about the impact of the *"Becoming a Band of Brothers"* retreat:

- This retreat was a ten on a ten point scale!
- You convinced me I need to stop trying to live the Christian live alone.
- Thanks for the practical suggestions about how to forge this kind of connection.

- When I get back from this retreat I am calling an old friend that I used to get together with to get connected as Check 6 brothers!
- As a pastor, I am convicted that I need to find a safe friend with whom I can build an accountability relationship.

G. Recognize that brokenness can also cause a man to realize his need for accountability. Although I challenge men to build brother-hood connections to prevent them from sliding down the steep slope of Internet pornography, sometimes it is the sliding down of that slope that awakens men to their need of some *Check 6* brothers. Here are the words of one pastor:

> Let me give you an update to encourage you about what's happened at DaySpring since the *Grace Transformed Sexuality* seminar that you led. As you know, DaySpring is filled with young men in their twenties and early thirties. This was certainly reflected in those that attended GTS. Prior to the seminar I knew that most of these guys struggled to some extent with pornography. And for the ones that are married I know from their wives the detrimental effect it is having on their young marriages. Heart breaking!
>
> Since the seminar we have determined the urgency of having a strong, committed ministry to our men. In fact we've determined that it is most likely the most important ministry to keep strong...and at the same time the most difficult to keep going. One of the men at the conference has stepped up and is taking the lead as our new Director of Men's Ministry. Our first order of business is to keep the conversation started at GTS alive. He and two other guys have volunteered to facilitate groups. Our goal is to create as many opportunities...times of day, days of the week, one on one's...whatever we have to do to get as many men talking about this as possible. Anyway...many, many, thanks.

In summary, the third way church leaders can help their men get connected, is to *continually cast a vision of brothers being connected*. We've just examined seven ways to do that. Though you can't program his friendship for him, **if you convince him that God wants to provide a Jonathan and David kind of connection for him,** he will be self-motivated to seek to forge such a brotherhood connection.

4. **Build strategically on already existing relationships.** Simply getting men who are already meeting to focus more on sharing their spiritual battles may be the most strategic path to helping the most men experience speak-the-truth-in-love relationships. If an existing men's Bible study decides to move from ninety percent content/ten percent prayer time to a fifty/fifty split with a focus on spiritual battles in both their discussion and prayer, they will experience deeper life-on-life connection.

Another way to get men better connected is to build on couple's home groups that already exist. Persuading the men and women to split into separate prayer groups for the last thirty-five minutes, at least once in a while, will help the men be more open about their spiritual battles. If the men were then asked to pick one spiritual battle for which they need prayer, the brothers would likely move to a deeper level of connection. Meantime, by splitting up this way, the same thing might be happening with the ladies.

One large church in Colorado Springs has organized the entire church around its adult Sunday school "communities." Bryan, the associate pastor responsible for men's ministry, is seeking to find men from each of those communities who have a vision for helping men get better connected. His way of thinking about getting hundreds of men connected is to build on the relationships that already exist in these adult Sunday school communities.

5. **Provide your men practical assistance connecting.** As we have seen, *Check 6* partnerships cannot be built from the top down. They are organic, real friendships that exist among men who want to be together. But this does not mean that the men's ministry team cannot help men to find other men working near them, living near them, or having a common interest with them. An effective men's ministry leadership team will be intentional about constantly trying to get its men better connected.

This mindset will cause the men's ministry leaders to shape everything in its ministry to assist men to better connect. They will have small group discussion as a part of nearly everything they do. A men's Saturday seminar will be designed with lots of discussion. Retreats will have plenty of time for discussion on the topic of our spiritual battles. One men's ministry team got permission from the deacons to shape the men's spring work day at their building to help men deepen their relationships. They provided lunch for everyone, but were intentional about asking the guys to sit together at the round tables so they could build relationships and get to know each other better.

A men's ministry point man from Virginia discovered the *Forging Bonds of Brotherhood* book. He took his leadership team through the book and passed it around to others. They spent eighteen months building *Check 6* relationships. Then, they invited me to speak at a Tuesday evening Beast Feast (barbeque) to cast a vision for men forging brotherhood bonds. To assist the men to forge such bonds, the leadership team bought a giant map of the Harrisonburg, VA area. As each man arrived for the dinner, he was asked to stick a different colored pin in the map: blue for where he lived, red for where he worked, and yellow for where he attended a men's study. This allowed the men in this church of a thousand to see which guys lived and worked near him.

Towards the end of the meeting, each man filled out a card indicating his interest in being in a study, having lunch with someone who worked nearby, etc. Then the leaders of various men's studies and lunches stood up to invite the other brothers into their group. Afterwards the men's leadership team looked over the cards and used the map to make practical suggestions to help men connect.

One lay men's ministry leader in Columbia, MD is so convinced of the power of Check 6 relationships that he has just taken it upon himself to personally connect men who work near each other with the challenge to start meeting together using the Check 6 questions for their agenda.

6. **Persevere.** Several years ago, I met a men's ministry pastor named Tom Beal from an amazing church in Annapolis, MD. This church had men's Bible studies out the kazoo. Tom told me they had about 200 men in men's studies (in a church of a thousand). I had already picked up on the fact that the male thing to do in this church was to be in a men's Bible study. I asked Tom, "How do you do it?"

He answered, "I have been here eleven years. It took me seven years of asking men to be in men's Bible studies over and over and over again. Finally, after about seven years the 'corporate culture' of the church began to change and our men just kind of expected to be in one of the Bible studies."

There is no quick, simple fix for the epidemic of male isolation the church faces today. Rome wasn't built in a day and neither are male friendships. But God is changing the DNA of the church. It will not change quickly, but you can have a part in helping men forge brotherhood connections in which they are *speaking the truth in love* and therefore are *growing up towards maturity into Christ the Head*.

Why Help Men Forge Bonds of Brotherhood? Final Thoughts

The next chapters of *Got Your Back* are yet to be written. There is no way such *speak-the-truth-in-love* connections can be programmed. But, as men are persuaded that God doesn't want them fighting their spiritual battles alone, and as their leaders model a commitment to this truth, God will inspire all kinds of creative ways for men to forge the brotherhood connections they need to grow up into Christ the Head. God is glorified by variety.

My prayer is that all of those who read this book will help defeat the epidemic of male isolation in today's church. The importance of getting men connected is nowhere stated more succinctly than in Ecclesiastes 4:10-12:

> *Two are better than one because they have a good return for their work: If one falls down, his friend can help him up. But pity the man who falls and has no one to help him up! Also if two lie down together, they keep warm. But how can one keep warm alone? Though one may be overpowered, two can defend themselves. A cord of three strands is not quickly broken.*

God, in his infinite wisdom, says it straight up. *"Two are better than one."* Solomon gives four reasons why. We need:

Mutual assistance when we are working. *"They have a good return for their work."* Christian men want to be faithful to Christ in fulfilling their heavy responsibilities. Almost any task is more easily accomplished by two than by one. We gain perspective by having somebody at our side. We have one to point out creative alternatives that we had not considered. We have someone to soften our hard edges, and someone to help bear the load.

Mutual encouragement when we are down. *"If one falls down, his friend can help him up. But pity the man who falls and has no one to help him up!"* Falling down and messing up is a way of life for us men. Sometimes, I think my life verse in the Bible is James 3:2, "We all stumble in many ways." That's us. We fall down so often that we need some brothers who are ready to pick us back up. Chuck Swindoll writes:

> You want the straight scoop? A lot of us tough guys sound strong, but the truth is we are weak. We sound like we've got it all together, but we don't. Take me... I have a small group of men who know me very well. They are trustworthy and confidential guys I really need. Why? Because I am weak and I need their counsel. Furthermore, I occasionally blow it. If you doubt that, take it by faith! I need these men to encourage me and, when necessary, to reprove me.[50]

Mutual support, when we are vulnerable. *"If two lie down together they keep warm. But how can one keep warm alone?"* Mountain climbers and soldiers understand this principle. Though their bodies are exposed to the hostile elements of cold and wind on three sides, the side turned toward a brother is protected from these raw elements, receiving, instead, the life-giving warmth they need.

On every side of his life, a man is met with a brutal reality—he must perform to be valued and loved. He needs one place where the warmth of Christ's unconditional love comes at him NO MATTER WHAT, even when his brothers see his sinful failure.

<u>Mutual protection when we are attacked</u>. *"Though one may be over-powered, two can defend themselves."* Christian men face an enemy who wants to steal and kill and destroy all that they count most precious. "For we do not wrestle against flesh and blood, but against the rulers, against the authorities, against the cosmic powers over this present darkness, against the spiritual forces of evil in the heavenly places" (Eph 6:12).

Two are better than one. I can think of no better way to summarize this passage in Ecclesiastes, and the message of this book than to quote Stu Weber, in *Locking Arms*.

> Together. It's one of the most powerful words in the English language. And geese know how to use it to full advantage. They seem to know instinctively that life is a team sport.
>
> Wildlife biologists tell us that a flock of geese, by flying in a 'V' formation, actually adds at least seventy-one percent more flying range than if each bird were flying on its own. As each bird flaps its wings, it actually creates an updraft for the bird immediately following. Left to itself, the lone goose experiences a drag and resistance that causes it to long for the flock. When the lead bird in the formation tires, it simply rotates back in the wing and another flies the point.
>
> Draft horses experience a similar, if earthbound, dynamic. Draft horses were made for pulling. Some years ago at a Midwestern county fair the champion animal pulled a sled weighted at forty-five hundred pounds. The second place animal dragged four thousand pounds. Then someone proposed harnessing the two big fellas together, to see what they could do as a team. Together, they pulled twelve thousand pounds!
>
> So let me ask the obvious. If our feathered friends know it, and the four-footed beasts experience it, why should we be so slow to learn it? Together is better. Especially, when hardship presses in. And there's a tough pull ahead.[51]

Group Discussion Guide

1. Before answering the discussion questions read through Appendix 1 and 2. What stood out to you about home leadership? What are your thoughts about the accountability questions?
2. Which of the practical suggestions for helping the men of your church to get connected seemed the most relevant for them? Explain.
3. Which aspects of Ecclesiastes 4:10-12 stand out the most to you? Why?

Check #1: What encouragements or successes have you had this past week?

Check #5: What non-believers are you building relationships with and how can I pray for your strategy to share Christ with them?

Check #6: What spiritual battles can I help you fight through my prayer for you?

3. Choose one of these options and share your preference with the group. **I would like to:**

   a) Keep meeting as a group, using a few of the *Check 6* questions.
   b) Keep meeting as a group but split into groups of 2-3 to go over some *Check 6* questions.
   c) Start meeting with one or two guys at another time to form a *Check 6* group.
   d) Another option.

4. Close this time with prayer.

Appendix 1

Check 6 Questions

Check #1:   What encouragements or successes have you had this past week?

Check #2:   What Biblical insight or verse from your quiet time has stood out to you recently?

Check #3:   What has been the most difficult part of being the spiritual leader at home lately?

Check #4:   Personal Accountability: Choose what you want your brother(s) to ask you about..

Check #5:   What non-believers are you building relationships with and how can I pray for your strategy?

Check #6:   What other spiritual battles can I help you fight through my prayer for you?

The PDF of these questions can be downloaded from the Store tab at www.forgingbonds.org under Got Your Back

Appendix 2

Further Questions about Leadership At Home

A. Which needs of your wife do you need to focus on meeting right now?

"Love" means making whatever sacrifice is necessary to meet the needs of another. It requires identifying the needs of the loved one. Here is a sample list that has been helpful to many men.

1. *Emotional intimacy with you.* This is the need to feel emotionally close to you. It is feeling one with you—like there are no barriers between you. It is feeling like you are her soul mate and best friend, with whom she constantly shares what is on her heart.
2. *Partnership with you on the home front.* This is her need to feel like she is not facing her responsibilities alone, but instead has a companion beside her sharing her cares and load.
3. *Spiritual intimacy with you, her spiritual leader.* A wife not only yearns to connect spiritually with her husband; she needs her husband to carry the weight of spiritual leadership so that she can flourish in her calling to be a suitable helper to him.
4. *Words of affirmation from you.* This is the need to know and hear repeatedly that she is highly valued by you, her husband—that her combination of beauty and feminine virtues is the perfect blend you need.

5. **Romance.** In her God-given feminine nature, a woman yearns to be swept off her feet, treated like a princess, and drawn into adventure. Romance, to her, is feeling cherished, valued, special, and pampered. Romance keeps her feelings for you at a constant warm level (which makes love-making more natural for her, since going from warm to hot is much easier than going from cold to hot).

6. **Female friends.** Wives, especially with small children at home, need regularly to be free from the kids to have adult conversations with other women. Women are relational creatures; they need meaningful connections with other women.

7. **Protection and rest.** Your role as a husband is to protect her from spiritual, emotional, and physical harm. Worrying about the kids safety, or the financial situation, wears on her.

8. **A secure home and secure finances.** A wife closely identifies herself with her home. The attention you give to your wife's honey-do-list is, to her, a reflection of the importance she has in your life. Also, her security is closely tied to your faithfulness in managing home and personal finances.

It is easy for a man to take his wife for granted so long as she doesn't spend too much, she keeps their home reasonably clean, they don't have too many fights, and sex is going okay. Such an attitude falls far short of our Lord's command to love her as he loves us! Add in our natural self-centeredness, and it is clear why we need to be regularly challenged by the brotherhood to keep setting the bar high.

B. What are you doing to disciple your kids?

We fathers have enormous influence in the lives of our children through our relationship with them and through fervent intercessory prayer on their behalf. Without brothers to keep us on track, however, we can easily waste the enormous potential we have to build into their lives, while they are in our homes. Instead of seizing this opportunity to invest time and energy to disciple our children, we allow our busy schedules, passivity on the home front, and spiritual laziness to steal this opportunity from us and our children. We can easily squander not only the chance to shape our own kids, but through them, to impact generations to come.

C. Do you need to change a bad attitude at home that is wounding others?

This is where the battle rages. We struggle with resentment when all that we do for the family is not appreciated or when our wives don't seem to care about our sexual needs. We are impatient with our wives and kids and may battle daily a sharp tongue that is quick to criticize and wound them. We easily tire of making ourselves listen to the details of our wife's day. We get angry when our kids are constantly irresponsible or when our wives have *their* agenda for *our* needed time to relax. It is in our homes where our selfish natures come out. That is why we need brothers to lift us up when we feel defeated, and impart strength to us for the battle through their friendship and intercession.

Appendix 3

Accountability Questions to Consider

Since our last meeting:

A. Have you taken time this week to bask in God's unconditional love for you?

John, who was known as Jesus' best friend, writes, "How great is the love the Father has lavished on us, that we should be called children of God! And that is what we are" (1 John 3:1). John teaches us the truth of adoption. Not only has God destroyed the barrier of guilt that separated us from himself by sending Christ to atone for our sin, he continues in his work of drawing us to himself through the cords of love by adopting us into his very family. In the strongest possible way, God is saying that he has done what is needed for us to be close to him. J.I. Packer observes,

> Justification is a FORENSIC idea, conceived in terms of LAW, and viewing God as JUDGE... But contrast this, now, with adoption. Adoption is a FAMILY idea, conceived in terms of LOVE, and viewing God as FATHER. In adoption, God takes us into his family and fellowship, and establishes us as his children and heirs. Closeness, affection, and generosity are at the heart of the relationship. To be right with God the JUDGE is a great thing, but to be loved and cared for by God the FATHER is a greater.[52]

Feasting on God's love meets the deepest yearnings of the masculine heart and helps me resist the idols (success, pleasure, respect, control, financial security, etc.) that seek to capture my heart. Abiding in Christ's love, as he commands me to (John 15:9-10), helps me love sin less and God more.

The prophet Zephaniah writes, "The LORD your God is with you, he is mighty to save. He will take great delight in you, he will quiet you with his love, he will rejoice over you with singing" (3:17). Scotty Smith challenges us to dwell on this truth:

What would it feel like in your heart to know that God not only *accepts* you, but that he richly *enjoys* you? To know that your company is his pleasure, your fellowship his joy, your face his delight? What effect would that have on how you think about God, yourself, others?[53]

B. As you look at the outward sins of your life, what is the sin beneath the sin? In other words, what idol has your heart been chasing lately?

Mankind's root problem is not merely an external, behavioral problem — it is an internal problem of the heart. One of the primary reasons human hearts are not more transformed is because the affections of people's hearts have been captured by idols that grip them and steal their hearts' affection away from God.

I may find myself unusually angry at my daughter for denting the car. A look beneath the surface reveals that the recent tight finances are making me depend on God, and I don't like that. I may explode at my wife when she asks about work. A little thought reveals my idol of success rearing its ugly head, not to mention the idol of wanting respect. I may indulge in lustful fantasy because my heart is bored and restless, needing the rush of sexual pleasure and release to be satisfied.

Since it is out of our hearts that evil comes, it is always valuable to consider what inner desire led to the outward behavior. As Calvin observed, the human heart is an idol factory. Usually, chasing an idol that promises to satisfy my heart is the sin beneath the sin. True repentance, then, means confessing that I have gone after another lover who promises to satisfy my heart. "You adulterous people," writes James. "Don't

124

you know that friendship with the world is hatred toward God? Anyone who chooses to be a friend of the world becomes an enemy of God" (4:4).

C. What aspect of Christ-like character do you see God wanting you to learn right now?

Romans 8:28 teaches us that all things work together for good for those who love God and who have been called **according to his purpose**. The last four words of this verse are the key to understanding how our painful, terrible trials can possibly be for our good—because those trials bring about **God's purpose** in our lives. Paul does not leave us in the dark about what that purpose is. He continues in vs. 29, *"For those he foreknew, he predestined to be **conformed to the likeness of his son**."* God's plan is to use our trials to accomplish his good purpose, which is conforming our character to the image of Christ.

So often the focus of our prayer is asking God to remove our difficult circumstances. While this is very appropriate, I believe he would be much more pleased if we asked him for the power to have the godly attitude he is seeking to build through our hard circumstances.

Galatians 5:22-23 tells us that the fruit of God's spirit at work in us is love, joy, peace, patience, kindness, goodness, faithfulness, meekness, and self-control. It is by this fruit being produced—us having these attitudes—that God is glorified. "By this is my father glorified," said Jesus, "that you bear much fruit and so prove to be my disciples." We need help learning to change the focus of our prayer to asking God to empower us with the godly attitudes that will glorify him.

D. Have you looked at sexually explicit material?

According to 60 Minutes, thirty years ago in America there were under a thousand X-rated movie theaters. Today, there are over eighty-three million, because of pornography piped into living rooms and family rooms through the Internet and cable TV. The first line of defense for Christian men seeking to remain sexually pure has always been to stay away from the stores where this stuff is available. The free-speech folks have now taken that line of defense from us.

Research reveals that the current rate of church-going men viewing Internet pornography is over 65%. *I do not see any way the church can effectively aid its men in battling this scourge, without getting them connected to other men at a deep enough level where they can provide accountability.* But to accomplish this goal, men must build friendships of support and trust.

In asking this question, be aware of what Joe White, calls, "the weasel factor." Men who have slipped in this area face an enormous temptation to find a way to weasel out of answering the question. They may change the wording, subtly skip over it, or dominate the agenda of the meeting so that the group doesn't get to it. Wise *Check 6* brothers prevent the weasel factor by always getting to the question and reading it exactly as it is.

E. Have you been too emotionally or physically close to a woman who is not your wife?

Rarely does a man have an affair out of the blue. Nearly always, he has been making subtle compromises in the areas of sexual boundaries for some time. So, we need to nip potential problems in the bud by setting clear boundaries and being held to that high standard by our brothers. I have a couple of rules that I follow concerning my secretaries. Though I might give a hug to some women in the church on some occasion, I have a rule that I don't touch my secretaries. I also have a rule that when it comes to friendship with a woman, either she is closer to my wife than to me, or I am closer to her husband than I am to her. Another boundary is to avoid having a female friend talking to you about the problems in her marriage. Refer the woman to your wife or another woman in the church.

Too physically close includes inappropriate hugs as well as sexual contact. It also normally includes being alone with a female work associate in her hotel room, or going out with her alone for a drink or a meal. Too emotionally close includes flirting, and permitting an emotional attachment to a female who becomes special. It is discussing subjects that are too personal, especially problems in each other's marriages. It is allowing yourself to get inappropriately close to a woman who is not your wife. This is where the battle to protect the sanctity of your marriage is fought. Affairs rarely start with sex. They begin with emotional closeness that is not appropriate for a married man.

F. Do you need to fix a broken relationship?

Paul commanded, *"Do not let the sun go down while you are still angry, and do not give the devil a foothold."* (Eph. 4:27) You and I cannot afford to stay angry with someone, because bitterness is an attitude that poisons our spiritual and emotional systems. Jesus with the same urgency, tells us to repair a relationship when someone is angry with us. *"Therefore, if you are offering your gift at the altar, and there remember that your brother has something against you, leave your gift there in front of the altar. First go and be reconciled to your brother; then come and offer your gift"* (Matt. 5:23-24).

G. Have you lied to anyone or been dishonest in your financial dealings?

When God says, "Above all," it gets my attention. He is obviously saying, "Make this top priority." In James 5:12, God says, *"Above all, my brothers, let your 'Yes' be yes, and your 'No,' no."* Keeping our word is elevated to top priority. Honesty is singled out and given the highest possible value.

Pragmatism reigns in twenty-first century America, and we bottom-line oriented men can easily cut moral corners and put our spin on the facts until they no longer tell the real story. The ends do not justify the means in God's economy. One of the best things we can do for each other as men is to keep challenging each other to operate on the basis of integrity.

End Notes

[1] Frank Broyles, *Brothers in Arms: A Journey From War to Peace,* (Austin, TX: University of Texas Press, 1996).

[2] This account of what happened was passed on to me by Joe Craft, the Executive Officer of the Basic School at Quantico Marine Base, Quantico, VA. Joe also explained the wingman relationship between two pilots. He left Quantico to command a Top Gun squadron at the Marine Corps Air Station, Miramar.

[3] Stu Weber, *Locking Arms: God's Design for Masculine Friendships* (Oregon: Multnomah Books, 1995), p. 77-78.

[4] The names in this true story have been changed to protect the participant's privacy.

[5] John Owen, *Sin and Temptation,* Classics of Faith and Devotions Series, (Oregon: Multnomah Books, 1986)

[6] Steve Childers, Spiritual Dynamics Class Notes, Reformed Theological Seminary, Orlando, 2005.

[7] John Eldrege, *Wild at Heart,* (Nashville: Thomas Nelson, 2001 Special Addition MIM), p. 157.

[8] This study, conducted by Promise Keepers, was quoted by Brian Doyle in a seminar he led at the National Coalition of Men's Ministries in Indianapolis in 2002.

[9] Stu Weber, *Locking Arms: God's Design for Masculine Friendships* (Oregon: Multnomah Books, 1995), p. 22

[10] David Smith, *The Friendless American Male* (Venura, CA: Gospel Light Publications, 1983), p. 96.

[11] Bob Hamrin, Great Dads Seminar.

[12] James 4:6, 1 Peter 5:5, Proverbs 3:34.

[13] Pat Morley, *The Man in the Mirror,* (Grand Rapids: Zondervan, 1989), p. 339.

[14] Randy Pope, *INsourcing: Bringing Discipleship Back to the Local Church,* (Grand Rapids: Zondervan, 2013), p. 66.

[15] Richard Phillips, *The Masculine Mandate,* (Orlando, Reformation Trust. 2010), p. 15.

[16] Larry Crabb, *The Silence of Adam*, (Grand Rapids: Zondervan, 1995) p. 11.

[17] ESV Study Bible, (Wheaton, IL: Crossway Bibles, 2008) p. 55.

[18] John Eldrege, *Wild at Heart,* (Nashville: Thomas Nelson, 2001 Special Edition MIM), p. 142.

[19] Stu Weber, *Tender Warrior: God's Intention for a Man*, (Sisters, OR: Multnomah Books, 1993) p. 171.

[20] Ibid.

[21] Robert Lewis, *The Quest for Authentic Manhood* Audio, (Little Rock, AR: Men's Fraternity, 2000).

[22] Philippians 2:3b

[23] Tom Joyce, *Vision Casting...To Infinity and Beyond,* CD, (Clarksburg, MD: Iron Sharpens Iron Conference, 2009), Disk 4.

[24] Chuck Colson, *Born Again*, (Grand Rapids: Baker, 1976), p. 337-339.

[25] Gene Getz, *Building Up One Another,* (Colorado Springs: David C. Cook, 1976), p. 7.

[26] Larry Crabb, *The Safest Place On Earth*, (Nashville: Thomas Nelson, 1999), p. 11.

[27] Chuck Swindoll, *Living Above the Level of Mediocrity* (Nashville: Thomas Nelson, 1989), p. 133.

[28] Pat Morley, *Man in the Mirror,* (Grand Rapids: Zondervan, 1989), p. 336.

[29] Letter from Chuck Miller.

[30] Robert Lewis, *The Quest for Authentic Manhood,* Audio, (Little Rock: Men's Fraternity, 2000).

[31] Joe Dallas, *Every Man's Battle Pastors Training* (Workshop Notes), New Life Ministries, 2003.

[32] Numerous sources attribute these words to Dr. James Dobson, which I believe came from a Focus on the Family Newsletter written in 1990.

[33] Pat Morley, *Man in the Mirror,* (Grand Rapids: Zondervan, 1989), p. 351.

[34] Acts 4:4

[35] Tom Joyce, *Vision Casting...To Infinity and Beyond CD* (Clarksburg, MD: Iron Sharpens Iron Conference, 2009) Disk 4.

[36] Dietrich <u>Bonhoeffer</u>, *Life Together,* (San Francisco: Harper, 1978).

[37] Randy Pope, *INsourcing: Bringing Discipleship Back to the Local Church,* (Grand Rapids: Zondervan, 2013), p. 46.

[38] Steve Gallagher, *At the Altar of Sexual Idolatry*, (Dry Ridge, KY: Pure Life Ministries, 1986), p. 68.

[39] Nate Larkin, Keynote Message (Gospel Man Conference: Atlanta, 2009).

[40] Tom Joyce, *Vision Casting…To Infinity and Beyond,* CD (Clarksburg, MD: Iron Sharpens Iron Conference, 2009), Disk 4.

[41] Dan Schawbel, *Millennials vs. Baby Boomers: Who Would You Rather Hire? (Time: Business and Money* <u>http://business.time. com/2012/03/29/millennials-vs-baby-boomers-who-would-you-rather-hire/</u>, March 29, 2012).

[42] Chuck Swindoll, *Living Above the Level of Mediocrity* (Nashville: Thomas Nelson, 1989), p. 137.

[43] John Eldrege, *Wild at Heart,* (Nashville: Thomas Nelson, 2001 Special Edition MIM), p. 177.

[44] Joseph Galloway and Harold Moore, *We Were Soldiers Once…and Young* (New York: Ballantine Books, 1992). p. xxii

[45] Ted Gluck and Dallas Jahncke, *Dalls and the Spitfire,* (Minneapolis: Bethany House, 2012).

[46] Stu Weber, *Tender Warrior: God's Intention for a Man* (Sisters, OR: Multnomah Books, 1993), p. 85.

[47] Don Sampson, Crossroads PCA, Woodbridge, VA

[48] Steve Brown, *What Was I Thinking: Things I've Learned Since I Knew It All* (New York: Howard Books, 2006), p. 108

[49] Peter Scazzero, *The Emotionally Healthy Church,* (Grand Rapids: Zondervan, 2003), p. 126.

[50] Chuck Swindoll, *Living On the Ragged Edge,* (Waco, TX: Word Books, 1985), p. 135.

[51] Stu Weber, *Locking Arms: God's Design for Masculine Friendships* (Sisters, OR: Multnomah Books, 1995), p 33.

[52] J. I.Packer, *Knowing God,* (Downers Grove, IL: InterVarsity Press, 1973), p. 187.

[53] Scotty Smith, *Objects of His Affection,* New York: Howard Books, 2005), p. 27.

About The Author

————— ❊ —————

DR. GARY YAGEL is the Executive Director of *Forging Bonds of Brotherhood*, and the Men's Ministry Advisor of the Presbyterian Church In America. He has served on the speaking faculty of *Man In the Mirror*, and spends his weekends speaking to men and coaching churches in men's discipleship. He has authored numerous books and currently teaches "Making Missional Disciples" at Reformed Theological Seminary, D.C. Gary and his wife, Sandy, have been married over thirty years, have five grown children, and reside in Olney, MD.

For further information about Gary's books or for free men's ministry resources go to www.forgingbonds.org.